STUDIES IN ENGLISH LITERATURE No. 17

General Editor

David Daiches

Professor of English in the School of English and American Studies,
University of Sussex

JOHN DONNE:
THE SONGS AND SONETS

by

A. J. SMITH

Senior Lecturer in English,
University College of Swansea

EDWARD ARNOLD (PUBLISHERS) LTD.
41 Maddox Street, London W.1

Printed in Great Britain by
The Camelot Press Ltd., London and Southampton

General Preface

It has become increasingly clear in recent years that what both the advanced sixth-former and the university student need most by way of help in their literary studies are close critical analyses and evaluations of individual works. Generalisations about periods or authors, general chat about the Augustan Age or the Romantic Movement, have their uses; but often they provide merely the illusion of knowledge and understanding of literature. All too often students come up to the university under the impression that what is required of them in their English literature courses is the referring of particular works to the appropriate generalisations about the writer or his period. Without taking up the anti-historical position of some of the American 'New Critics', we can nevertheless recognise the need for critical studies that concentrate on the work of literary art rather than on its historical background or cultural environment.

The present series is therefore designed to provide studies of individual plays, novels and groups of poems and essays, which are known to be widely studied in Sixth Forms and in universities. The emphasis is on clarification and evaluation; biographical and historical facts, while they may of course be referred to as helpful to an understanding of particular elements in a writer's work, will be subordinated to critical discussion. What kind of work is this? What exactly goes on here? How good is this work, and why? These are the questions which each writer will try to answer.

DAVID DAICHES.

Contents

1. *Invention*

A sense of the quick nerve of quotidian experience is remarkable enough in lyric poetry to account for at least some part of the enthusiasm Donne's *Songs and Sonets* have excited in the last fifty years. A live openness to the momentary stir of street and chamber is a character of the theatre; it suggests the brutal *tour de force* of the empathic imagination by which Ben Jonson energises his world of 'Love, cosenedge, flatterie, bawderie, slye conveighance of whordome', with its 'cookes, queanes, knaves, baudes, parasites, courtezannes, lecherous old men, amorous young men . . . of infinite varietie.'[1] And the *Songs and Sonets* have more positive qualities in common with Renaissance comedy than a sensitivity to the texture of surrounding circumstances. It has been a common experience of these poems that they offer one an entrée to a diverse world, alive with a variety of mordantly vivid situations, and furnished with the myriad objects and properties of current traffic; a world, like Jonson's, at once exhilaratingly unfamiliar and disconcertingly like our own.

True it is an artificially restricted world; as in another way the world of *The Alchemist* and *Bartholomew Fair* is restricted. Only whereas those works are full of people on the make and their dupes, and are closely focused on exaggerated self-seeking in a variety of manifestations, the *Songs and Sonets* treat exclusively of love; or more strictly, of amorous relationships between the sexes. That in itself is not remarkable for its time. From the thirteenth century lengthy works were devoted exclusively to the anatomy of love. Dante's *Vita Nuova* is one. The most directly influential body of lyric poetry in European literature, the *Canzoniere* of Petrarch consists of some three hundred and eighty sonnets, madrigals and *canzoni*, sensitively registering every nuance of the poet's forty-seven-year devotion to one Laura. The sixteenth century itself saw the development, after Petrarch, of the amorous sonnet sequence; and the English poetic renaissance was heralded in 1557 by the publication of a collection of love-lyrics called, specifically, *Songes and Sonettes*.

[1] Stephen Gosson, *Playes confuted in Five Actions* (1582).

Petrarchan sequences present the affective drama of a single character; the same man experiencing a set round of feelings in a variety of situations. The *Songs and Sonets* give a more inherently theatrical impression. They exhibit a seemingly unfocused diversity of experiences and attitudes, sometimes indeed contradictory attitudes, and a free range of feelings and moods. The mode is dynamic rather than static; less like a photograph album than a high-speed review.

Nor are the disclosures presented as Browningesque monologues, in which a string of factitiously individualised characters perform so as to focus their own idiosyncrasies. It is part of the art and discipline of these poems that the 'I' who speaks is not only a distinctive personality but also, whatever the inconsistencies, recognisably the same *persona*; a commentator who, far from holding himself up for sympathy or judgment, so removes his own quirks from our detached scrutiny that he persuades us momentarily to see things through his eyes, to entertain his consciousness as ours. But this is an 'I' of protean range of experience and attitudes, a kind of walking conspectus of all the feelings, short of servility, that men are apt to have towards women at one time or another. So that participation is likely to be more than an academic matter.

The most conspicuous singularity of the whole output is precisely its tang of reality, in the sense that it seems to reflect life in a real rather than a poetical world. The traditional decorum of love-poetry formalises a cult of opulent beauty which takes the accumulation of precious properties as appropriate correlative of the emotion. Petrarch's own call for a style totally removed from the vulgar and plebeian[1] fixed humanist notions of stylistic decorum which became prescriptive in sixteenth-century Europe, and recommended themselves to most serious writers of Donne's own day: 'The further one departs from the common and ordinary usage, the more refinement and the more delight one acquires; and this is the difference between verse and prose.'[2] By these ideals Donne's properties make a bizarre list. There are conventional counters, of a sort, in profusion: eye-beams, tears, sighs, love-tokens and the like. But they take on a brisk life in a mental activity which is just as likely to call in coins, or bullets, or maps, or post-mortem examinations, or legal sharp practice, or the plague, or a disreputable street incident, or some maxim of state. The absence of conventional sentiment is likewise patent

[1] *De Rebus Familiaribus*, 10:4:2.
[2] F. Sommo, *Discorso in difesa del metro nelle Poesie* (Padova, 1601), 13ʳ.

at times. To make a flea the central property of a lovers' dialogue seems by courtly lights as indecorous as it is possible to be, however faithful to the actuality of a sixteenth-century wooing. If love in Dante is an idealised abstraction from reality for the sake of truth to a higher or more inward reality, Donne seems chiefly concerned with the texture of actuality itself.

The inclusiveness of the *Songs and Sonets* has likewise much occupied modern critics. Inclusiveness was a quality which interested the early humanists, who were witnessing for themselves the power of literary works to encapsulate a whole civilisation for posterity; a concern Donne recalls with characteristic exaggeration:

> When this booke is made thus,
> Should againe the ravenous
> Vandals and Goths inundate us,
> Learning were safe; in this our Universe
> Schooles might learne Sciences, Spheares Musick, Angels Verse.
> *(A Valediction: of the booke)*

A faith so deeply confirmed by experience inevitably affected practice, in a way which wasn't wholly consonant with notions of stylistic decorum simultaneously held. Sixteenth-century scholiasts professed to find in Dante and Petrarch a summary of philosophy, metaphysics, mathematics, astronomy, and the natural sciences, and produced detailed evidence from the poems to substantiate the claim. And they went further. Conceiving the poetic *genres* as imitating the settled modes of experiencing, and ordering experience, they held a great poet to be one who sums up all human awareness in a given field. For love, the paradigm was Petrarch; and the *Canzoniere* was invested with a high purpose as offering a model of man's search for a moral absolute, a Dantean quest in which Laura plausibly figures as 'the universal idea of beauty and delightfulness' to whom all perfections in common are assigned.[1] At a humbler level, Petrarch was studied as 'the grand master both for practice and science of all the amorous passions',[2] whose sequence 'comprehended in itself the entire possibility of a spiritual diary', and is 'the deposit of every proof and experience of love'.[3]

[1] B. Tomitano, *Ragionamenti Della Lingua Toscana* (Venezia, 1545), 116[r].
[2] L. Domenichi, *Dialogo d'amore* (Venezia, 1562), p. 38.
[3] G. Spagnoletti, *Il Petrarchismo* (Milano, 1959), pp. 22-23.

Petrarch's real achievement has to do with the definitive subtlety of his exploration of a more limited area of experience; but expositors also pointed to the inventive fertility, not to say virtuosity, called for in the contrivance of a staggering number of poetic devices, all distinct and all vitally interesting. The evidence suggests that it was this last feat which elicited most labour and art. In a number of places Petrarch himself advises that a poet's business is to be like a bee, accumulating and ordering excellences from every conceivable literary source to turn into his own honey; and he left it on record that this was his own practice.[1]

The legend of Petrarch's reworking of material from the Roman poets and his own Italian predecessors hardened by the early sixteenth century into a working principle of Imitation, whose practical results were the institution of Petrarch himself as the pattern of lyric verse in the vulgar, and the exhaustive codification of his devices and locutions for the use of poets. The 'petrarchism' which ensued produced great poetry as well as wastes of dead wood all over Europe. But its basis was a discipline repugnant to modern ideas, the acceptance of an exacting and far-reaching decorum of love-verse whose prior requirement was the acknowledgment of a pool of recognised usages, challenging a poet by the very frequency of their recurrence to 'make them his own' in a definitive reworking: 'for emulation is always conjoined with imitation'.[2]

The obligation thus understood was seen, and prescribed for, rather as an opportunity than a fetter. Thus it was as guide not arbiter that G. C. Scaliger opened his authoritative account of lyric poetry with a long list of the themes love-poets have generally used, a list which takes in a number of situations in the Songs and Sonets.[3] Any of the European lyric sequences of the day parades whole repertories of stock motifs, more or less artfully assimilated—the aube, valediction, dirge, curse, threat of revenge, aubade, and a score more. Sidney, Donne's master as well as his foil, takes up devices to be found in any number of French and Italian poets from Cavalcanti to Tasso, and his assignable re-uses alone run into dozens. It wasn't felt that such debts should be hidden; quite the contrary. The anticipation of an unsophisticated audience seems to have driven Sidney's artless precursor Thomas Watson to appear in print

[1] De Rebus Familiaribus, 22:2:16 et passim.
[2] P. Bembo, in a letter to G. F. Pico, De Imitatione, c. 1512.
[3] Poetices Libri Septem (Vincentius, 1561), Book 3.

with the origins of his devices indicated, and sometimes even quoted
for direct comparison:

> Seraphine in his Strambotti hath many prettie inventions concerning
> the Lookingglasse of his Mistress; wherwence many particulars of this
> passion are cunningly borrowed, part beeing out of one place and part
> out of another.[1]

Donne's general attitudes are not Petrarch's or Sidney's, let alone
Watson's. But it is demonstrable that the *Songs and Sonets* draw heavily
on the current repertory; as indeed on a variety of European sources,
common or esoteric. Materially, they testify as does petrarchism itself
to a mental habit unchallenged in Europe until the quantitative science
of the seventeenth century. For Donne as for Dante and for the inter-
vening centuries, knowledge was an *a priori* order, something already
delivered and fixed which only needed systematic classification in vast
thesauruses and compendia to be at anyone's disposal who was adroit
enough in managing the properties by which it was discriminated.
Every created thing, or class of things, was conceived to be endowed
with its own unalterable characteristics, and these were known: it is
the nature of the crocodile to weep, of the camomile to grow more the
more it is trodden on, of the Frenchman to be fantastic, and so on:

> herbes kepe their vertue of necessitie. The Adamant draweth iron,
> even by nature. And so the bloud stone stoppeth blood. . . .[2]

New ideas were assimilated to established categories, and passed into
currency as common coin. Donne's own citation of 'new Philosophy'—
the recent revolutionary astronomical theories—as latest instance of the
uncertainty and vanity of human sciences is a case in point.[3]

The order was institutionalised in the academic disciplines of thought
and expression, whose ends were civic oratory, legal pleading, and
theological controversy. Renaissance logic and rhetoric were not instru-
ments of inquiry, or even of plain communication, but set means of
redisposing what was known to give it the utmost persuasive or pro-
batory force. Fundamental to all their argumentative and many of their
stylistic devices was the exploitation of the correspondences between the

---

[1] *Ekatompathia* (1582), No. xxiv.
[2] Thomas Wilson, *The Rule of Reason* (1551), L.ii^r.
[3] *The first Anniversary*, line 205.

properties of things—as for example in syllogisms, or ingenious analogies:

> *Similitude* . . . is a likeness when two thynges or mo then two, ar so compared and resembled together, that thei both in some one propertie seme like. . . . Therefore those that delite to prove thynges by similitudes, must learne to know the nature of diverse beastes, of metalles of stones and al suche, as have any vertue in them, and be applied to mannes life.[1]

One scarcely needed to discover such tendentious correspondences for oneself. Since commonplace matter was everywhere marshalled precisely by properties in the so-called 'places' of logic—Cause, Effect, Form, Sensible Qualities, and the like—thesauruses would have already grouped together hundreds of objects with like attributes, and one had merely to look up the appropriate 'place' to find ample store from which to draw. Centuries of resort to the same categories, or 'places', for the same ends made the resulting accumulation of commonplace counters almost a cryptic language. An artist with a coterie following in particular, such as most Renaissance audiences were, could rely on a readiness to supply a web of related circumstances which might give point to a usage or make it intelligible.

Iconography yields relevant instance. The emblem-mode was the external expression of an inherently qualitative concern with phenomena, and part of the essential texture of Renaissance thought and ceremonial. It consituted a kind of visual language of hieroglyphics, sometimes highly esoteric, in which a representation is offered less for any dramatic force it might have than for what it means, emblematically, to the man who can read the symbolic properties and interpret their intricate juxtapositions. Thousands of these emblems or emblematic properties were established in common usage, and ultimately standardised in huge glossed compendia. To glance through one of these, or at such practical assemblages as the four hundred or so emblematic frescoes covering the upper walls of the Council Hall in Padua,[2] is to find a furniture very like Donne's—globes, retorts, callipers, scales, rings, circles, gold, wells,

---

[1] Thomas Wilson, *The Arte of Rhetorique* (1553), F. 101^{v-r}.

[2] Il Salone della Ragione, decorated under the supervision of Giotto in the early fourteenth century.

sundials, phoenixes, suns, primroses, eagles, all carrying multiple emblematic import.

Donne's compasses have a typical history. The figure is common in early use with the general import of regular rule and rectitude, a sense deepened by the association with the circle, emblem of perfection and eternity. When the Plantin Press adopted it as their imprint in the mid-sixteenth century the moral sense, at least, had hardened into the meaning the Press motto announces, *Labore et Constantia*—glossed in one English emblem-book as resolute constancy and perseverance.[1] It was the poet-dramatist Guarini who in a madrigal of the 1580s fixed the emblem for a situation elaborated long before from Petrarch. He made it exact embodiment of the valedictory assurance that in physical separation the lovers' hearts will remain one and keep them firm, so that their return to the starting point will be the completion of a desire to which absence is no more than the means.[2] Here is the prose sense of Guarini's madrigal: 'I am always with you, agitated but firm; and if the more I leave you the less I run away, then I am like the compass, keeping always one foot in you as my firm centre while the other suffers the rotations of fortune. But fortune cannot bring it about that I don't girate about you.'

This easy commerce between thing and idea is typical of an outlook which sometimes seems barely concerned with the difference between a figurative and a literal sense. To develop as if it were literally true the figurative claim that separated lovers carry each other's hearts, thus preserving each other from alteration and from death too, was one of a mass of 'conceited' possibilities offered for a love poet's individual exploitation. Many were simple materialisations worked up from Petrarch, whose own elaborate conceits had embodied a penetration well beyond the capacity of most petrarchans. Tears caused floods and drowned people; sighs devastated the earth; sighs and tears together brought about shipwrecks; eyes ignited or killed people. Others were paradoxes or vast hyperboles, again at bottom often enshrining a true perception but burying it under the fine flourish of the extravagance. The mistress aggregates in herself the world's riches; all past beauties, and all

[1] G. Wither, *A Collection of Emblemes Ancient and Modern* (1635), Book 3.
[2] A Florentine *canzona* of about 1506, 'Donna, contra a la mia voglia', offers a typical presentation of the developed conceit. This piece had a curious fame as the favourite song of Cesare Borgia. It is given in W. H. Woodward, *Cesare Borgia* (1913), p. 427.

the lover's past pleasures, were only a shadow or imperfect anticipation of her; true lovers become one being and have no separate identity or existence; the mistress's absence or illness causes the foliage to wither, and her death brings about the decay and moral collapse of the whole world, as well as the annihilation of the lover. Or a poet might attempt a quizzing of amorous relationships, or of his own fortunes in love, under the show of one or another stock proceeding: he could declare that love as he now practises is a usurper and no true god, seek to define love, bid a disillusioned farewell to love, or whatever. There was a real language here in which true things could be said; but in a situation where freshness tended to be equated with greater extravagance, figurative plays readily took on a life of their own, as ingenious anecdote or chop-logic, and became a sterile way of making with the blocks.

Before Donne reached manhood Tasso was complaining of the vanity of poets who claimed that their mistress's eyes were arquebuses on wheels, and her eyebrows Turkish Arches, or who feigned that Charon made a boat of the arrows launched at him by love, and plied it on the river of his tears.[1] Nearly a century before that again, the hyperbolic possibilities of figurative conceits had been exploited to the limit in Italy, by Neapolitan court poets seeking new gestures of praise. Antonio Tebaldeo has so many arrows in his breast from his lady's eyes that the blind god carries him in mistake for his quiver. Serafino D'Aquila's hot sighs fry the birds in the air; and his ardours fire first his clothes and then the sea he leaps into, which beats against the rocks and ignites them too. His mistress's eyes shatter mirrors, or reflected back from a mirror, ignite themselves. He proves in himself a whole hagiology of the miracles of love, among them the fact that his icy mistress lives securely, salamander-like, in the furious combustion of his heart. He has together in his heart gold from Cupid's finer arrows, the live image of the Marchesa of Mantua, and fire; and these coming together mint and coin enough tear-medallions bearing her image to make half the world blessed.

A less mechanical mode is the juggling with ideas typically essayed by the Spaniard Chariteo, who offers such dialectical exercises as a demonstration that he will be far better off in Hell than now, and in fact uniquely blessed there. His sonnet 'Voi, donna' asserts that he and his mistress will go to Hell together, she for pride, he for too great ambition

[1] *Del Poema Eroico*, in *Prose* ed. F. Flora (Milano, 1935), p. 528.

in daring to aspire to a celestial thing. But while she will be in greater torment than the damned, having him for company, he will be in paradise gazing on her; more than paradise, since he will be the one blessed soul among the damned. Nor will the damned spirits be able to harm him, since the only way of tormenting him will be by denying him the sight of Hell.

If such inversions of ordinary sense carry paradox to risible extreme, they are not all wanton indulgence. Behind the mad extravagances, often enough, lies the level-headed work of formal and even delicate recommendation of public virtues; and the inventions themselves are the postures of the court poet fulfilling his due office of praise and celebration in the expected lyric mode of witty hyperbole. The artificiality, and the preciousness, are the stamp of a particular fashion of coterie writing. What is stable is the indirect advancement of a quite sober sense through the exhilarating intricacy of a witty play.

Individuation

The natural disposition of readers from Isaac Walton on to take Donne's poems as the spontaneous outcome of unique moments of feeling, and self-awareness, convincingly testifies to their radically differentiated life. This is a quality that shows up most obviously in the handling of like themes. *A Valediction: of my name, in the window*, and *A Valediction: of the booke* have a similar movement and tone, but they differ sharply in device, and in the kind of inventive virtuosity developed from it. *Breake of day*, another valediction, purports to be the outcry of a woman—in itself no innovation in love poetry; while *The Expiration*, unlike all the rest, is an enactment of the very moment of parting which gets its force from the explosive vehemence this climax releases. *A Valediction: of weeping* and *A Valediction: forbidding mourning* invite subtler comparison by posing parallel difficulties which turn alike on the proper behaviour of lovers at parting. Yet they are wholly unlike, both because of the extreme dissimilarity of form and device, and because they make exactly opposite assumptions; a case where the disputant's feat of pleading opposite sides of a question with equal conviction seems to have been raised to a higher level, as a means of implying the equivocalness of experience.

The pursuit of a very much handled motif through some half-a dozen pieces, so vividly individualised, suggests a degree of conscious virtuosity which is the rule rather than the exception in late Renaissance art; a design which the archetypal example of Michelangelo shows to be consistent with the highest seriousness. The brilliances of mannerist painters have their poor equivalent in the frantic ingenuities of the English sonneteers of the 1590s, with their largely barren cleverness in rearranging the properties:

> How often hath my pen (mine heart's Solicitor!)
> Instructed thee in Breviat of my case!
> While Fancy-pleading eyes (thy beauty's Visitor!)
> Have patterned to my quill, an angel's face.[1]

At very least the *Songs and Sonets* are distinguished from that by the quality of the consciousness they engage.

In a lyric by Donne an entire dramatic circumstance is realised, and evoked from the outset by the pitch of the address:

> Marke but this flea, and marke in this,
> How little that which thou deny'st me is;
> > (*The Flea*)

The scene is called up, peopled, and tensed by the single speaking voice, and the poem goes on as though an action unforeseen at the start were evolving there and then, which the reader follows through a spontaneous commentary on it spoken by one of the participants. It is the method of these poems to present one side of a dramatic dialogue, in which attack and tone are relied upon to evoke the other party and control the distance between the persons, telling us implicitly how they stand towards each other. This is a fiction which does much to give Donne's lyrics their peculiar immediacy, as well as their intensity, and whose set he varies and adjusts with sensitive precision. The means are often unobtrusively slight. Nothing so pungently urges the actuality of the situation in *The Dreame*, in the teeth of scores of previous handlings of the motif, as the quiet shift into the present tense in the third stanza. It is as though the events there hadn't taken place when the poem opened, and the stanza itself were the live reaction to them, a rejoinder whose dialectical subtlety, carrying the main interest, is thus made to seem anything but a cold sleight-of-mind.

Nor is it only the action which evolves. A celebrated insight of Mario

---

[1] Anon, *Zepheria* (1594), canzon 20.

Praz avers that Donne's poetry offers us the rhythm of thought itself.[1] The simulation of the live movement of the mind is what distinguishes poems like *The Extasie*, or *Lovers infiniteness* from more orthodox invocations. George Herbert's *The Collar* is magnificently dramatic, but it narrates a movement which has already taken place and been completed—a past event. Whereas the stages of *The Extasie* give the appearance of having been reached there and then, as though the movement forward of the poem is itself the immediate development of the poet's thought and awareness—'But O alas, so long, so farre. . . .' Donne's characteristic twists, turns, reversals here carry force beyond their dialectical life. They suggest the restless activity of the mind, perpetually probing and spontaneously revising its own affirmations. *Lovers infiniteness* abruptly disappoints the expectation the whole earlier movement has raised, with a sudden reversal of thought which is in fact presented as the leap to a fresh implication. He was anxious that their contract should allow him all her love, nervously aware of the possible legal quibbles by which she might evade it; and then abruptly he doesn't want so much after all as it strikes him that his larger end would be defeated by a premature finality.

This pattern of sudden reversal of an expectation deliberately aroused, followed by a paradoxical justification, is as near a formula as one finds in Donne; but there is nothing mechanical about it. The expected (and conventional) degodding of Cupid in *Loves Deitie* is abruptly abandoned: 'Rebell and Atheist too . . .'. In cold terms, an incomplete awareness, pointing one way, is suddenly overthrown by a clearer judgment, so that the final outcome reverses the apparent trend of the poem. But as it emerges this is less a dialectical twist than the live enactment of a whole human circumstance in which such transitions manifest themselves through rich and subtle modulations of mood; from sardonic exasperation to menace, and then abruptly to shocked realisation of his own awful treason and blasphemy.

The vibrant dramatic life of *The Canonization* derives in part from continual shifts of attack, conveyed through modulations of grammatical mood; a kind of dramatic syntax. In this as in *Song*, 'Goe, and catche', and *The Expiration*, it is by the device of the wholly unrealised other person that the poem develops as a stream of shifting injunctions, and in fact

[1] *John Donne* (Torino, 1958), p. 272.

presents nothing more in itself than the varying and justification of the mood of the address in the given situation. This care for nuance of mood can be more subtly dramatic. The delicate fluctuation between challenge, threat, and invitation in *The Dampe* is carried in adjustments of conditional and imperative which, beyond setting up a dramatic pattern of suspense and resolution, present a living complex of attitudes and motives, modulating sensitively as fresh possibilities strike in. The dramatic syntax of *The Anniversarie*, a most delicately wrought structure of rhetorical patterning and syntactical modulation, powerfully conveys an impression of immediacy, of the mind working keenly and sensitively there and then. Here, the overall movement from assurance to regret and irresolution, and then upward to reassurance and doubly confident celebration, is directly realised in the syntax as the underthought of a lover in conversation with his mistress. It is a picture of an intricate and delicate movement of the mind, extended by dramatic embodiment into a kind of complex gesture; a convincing simulacrum of the subtle flux of consciousness which makes up human thought.

Orthodox petrarchan attitudes were susceptible of a degree of dramatic presentation because they assumed a rhetorical end and an implicit dialectic. The lover addressed or apostrophised something—a sympathetic overhearer, the lady's glove or her dog, Love himself. In the *Songs and Sonets* the address becomes a central instrument of dramatic life; not a cold apostrophe but a means of directly involving a world of people and objects, from the poet's own heart to representative onlookers and the activities of whole sects. These continual second personal invocations colour and diversify, as well as crowding the stage. Each distinct address fixes its own degree of tension and carries its own piquant nuance of attitude—brusque detachment, comically patronising pity, sombre warning or menace, cavalier panache.

But in these poems addressing someone is not like writing a letter to them. Late sixteenth-century dramatists learned to exploit the casual discovery, taking one at once into the middle of an action already going forward, and inviting one to pick up the threads from clues obliquely dropped:

> In sooth, I know not why I am so sad:
> It wearies me; you say it wearies you;

This is just Donne's entry:

> I wonder by my troth, what thou, and I
> Did, till we lov'd?
> > (*The Good-morrow*)

A casual aside, a sudden insight, a snatched reassurance in the moment of parting, is made to evoke a circumstance which the overhearer has to piece out as in life:

> Sweetest love, I do not goe,
> For wearinesse of thee,
> > (*Song*)

The poem, strictly, is presented as the speech of the lover, a stream of injunctions mingled with meditative asides and comments; and it is through this seemingly total enactment of the consciousness of the leading participant that the situation is evoked, the issue between them loaded, and the poem held dramatically taut.

The opening of *The Expiration* fixes at once an exact moment of physical action and extreme emotional stress:

> So, so breake off . . .

We have come upon him unequivocally in the act of pulling himself back from the kiss, and holding off her desperate attempts to prolong this last embrace; a vivid little scene fixed in the first eight words. The whole of the poem following is in fact a series of imperatives and justifications of some grammatical complexity, whose effect is to enact alive his own attempts to convince himself of the necessity of their parting, or to make the best of it; motions which imply together both her extreme unwillingness to let him go, and his struggles with himself. The evocative power of the slightest signal when so loaded dramatically comes out in the repetition of 'Goe'. He has just asked her to 'Turne thou ghost that way', and assumed that with her immediate compliance they will be spared the pain of a formal farewell or a forced leavetaking. The effect of the second 'Goe' is to undo this at once. It is necessary to say the word after all, she hasn't turned away; he has to make her do so, to force himself from her and her from him. The simple reiteration evokes the manifold struggle which the rest of the poem conceitedly develops, its chop-logic thus given live dramatic point.

Such finesse is far from artless, but this isn't an art that obtrudes. On the contrary, motivation often seems riskily tenuous. *The Canonization* enacts a particularly vehement confrontation, but we are left to infer from the response what kind of wiseacre is addressed, crucial as that is; and also to pick up the ironic twist by which this shadowy lay-figure is finally drawn into the action and made to utter to the poet and his mistress the invocation which is the rebuttal of his own (again understood) objections.

These bystanders conveniently populate the *Songs and Sonets*, now the peg for a representative attitude or motive, now the means of eliciting some central declaration. The impression of a dramatic situation so tangibly circumstantial that the poet can take it for granted, or evoke it with the slightest hint, is strengthened by still more covert uses of person, which exploit an ambiguity, control shifts of addressee or switches of attack, play off the parties against each other. *The broken heart* actually moves through the gradual localisation of the persons as the poem advances—the uncertainty until the third stanza of the person addressed—and then turns on the difference between the conjectured motives of that person and the actual actions of Love. *The Will* draws in a vast number of human types, but develops as a second-personal address to Love until the last stanza, when a quiet swerve from 'thou' to 'your' shows us that the scornful mistress has been there all the time, presumably receiving the oblique affronts in her face; an effective reorientation of the poem, almost a fresh dramatisation, which is fixed entirely in the distinction between 'thou' and 'you', Love and the mistress. The declamatory conviction of *A Feaver* gets home partly because of some stark switches of address after the third stanza. Here the opening establishes an impassioned but distanced mode of second-personal address, almost as if to lull the reader and leave him more open to the shock of the violent break from it in the fourth and fifth stanzas— 'O wrangling schooles,'; a cry followed up by an observation treating her as a third party, before he returns to the earlier mode. So that the poem seems in fact to move through a series of violent dramatic impulses —an impassioned address to the sick mistress, exclamatory cry to the world, a momentary reflection or aside to the audience as it were, and then a return, reassured, to her. In *The Indifferent* there is a matter of subtle juggling with personal pronouns, which plays off the motives at issue between the poet, the heretics in love, and Venus. In this succession of subtly implicit shifts of addressee 'you' now appears to be a whole

series of potential mistresses, now the poet himself; and the last five
lines are in fact Venus's address to him:

> alas, Some two or three
> Poore Heretiques in love there bee,
> Which thinke to stablish dangerous constancie.
> But I have told them, since you will be true,
> You shall be true to them, who'are false to you.

The twist lies in the fact that 'you', finally, is not the poet but what
Venus is reporting to him that she has said to the heretically constant
women—and of course in the logic-chopping revenge Venus, and the
poet, devise for them. It is the essence of such expedients that they don't
offer the reader a puzzle, as they easily might; rather, they suggest their
quite complicated relationships by quiet indirection.

The peculiarly rich representation of life accessible to this mastery of
dramatic rhetoric is felt rather than remarked in *The Good-morrow*,
where Donne plays on modulations of mood and person as delicately as a
lutenist. This is a dramatic counterpoint, complicating the sensitive
movement of a man's thought with the interplay of two separate wills.
Hesitations, adverse possibilities, momentary resolutions, sudden
certainties, appear as the reflexes of an address which constantly flickers
between individualness and union; and the rhetoric is sensitive enough to
suggest a concerted affirmation with continual qualifying asides, as well
as to carry alive in the diction the very process of separate identities
merging into one-ness, then pulling apart again, and finally coming
confidently together:

> If our two loves be one, or, thou and I
> Love so alike, that none doe slacken, none can die.

It is another means by which a poem is made to enact its own meaning.

Whatever areas of experience lie beyond the reach of an art that
eschews the discipline of a traditionally refined decorum, the *Songs and
Sonets* have little of the claustrophobic constriction of genre poetry; they
impress one less as artificial literature than as the extension of a living and
alert consciousness. Donne never lets us forget the world outside the
poem. No gesture he makes and no attitude he strikes inhibits any part
of his contact with the world's life, and sometimes a low order of life:

(For graves have learn'd that woman-head
To be to more than one a Bed)
(*The Relique*)

Courtly attitudes, separating the public from the private order, imply a
dominant passion by which nothing else has any interest for the poet at
all. The *Songs and Sonets* rather suggest a sceptical mind, embroiled in
the stir of practical affairs, among which the *affaire de cœur* takes its place
on equal terms and unforcedly refers beyond itself:

Now as those Active Kings
Whose foraine conquest treasure brings,
Receive more, and spend more, and soonest breake:
(*The Dissolution*)

The shrewd political analogy claims at least equal interest with the
private state it purports to elucidate; possibly too much for so slight a
truth.

The world is present in another sense too. Even a rather abstract and
mechanical piece like *The Paradox* peoples its scene by a manifold
personal reference, giving a sense of freedom (and hence of reality) in
time and in the world of people. This is a sense *The Will* notably enlarges
of a real and tangible situation, where even in an apostrophe to love a
man can look back, and forward, and naturally summon a variety of
people as they occur to him, bringing the human types swarming in as
exuberantly as at Bartholomew Fair. The effect of the sudden turn
to the mistress in the last stanza, a stroke also essayed in *The Funerall*, is that the lover has maintained through the poem the insulting
fiction of a speech to another person in disregard of her, only casually
dropping it at the end to let the reader see as much. This is a
condition where a poem begins to feel like a total enactment, at
which the reader only adventitiously looks on. Its import is that
Donne writes a lyric poem through with a fully realised set of dramatic particulars in his mind, not only what he calls in but the
accessory circumstances too; as Stanislavski in producing Chekov's
Seagull is said to have realised the entire Sorin household and estate, and
got his actors to traverse the appropriate paths in their minds before they
entered the small bit of it depicted on the stage. The poem emerges as a
speech out of the middle of a moving action, modified by its surround-
ings and referring spontaneously to them. Hence the feeling these lyrics

repeatedly give, not only of vivid particularity, but of density; of rich life spreading out from the poem, and external circumstances bearing in on it.

Originality

Donne's originality is bound up with his use of common positions, an awareness of which he sometimes patently assumes. But its warrant is just the quality of his imagination. One can say accurately that *The Apparition* recombines several stock motifs—the lover's death of his mistress's disdain, the midnight visitation, and the revenge or curse. What matters more is that it is an intensely realised whole, a vivid personation which is dramatically of a piece, from the tense hissing deliberateness of tone and movement to the livid sharpness of the night-mare scene:

> Bath'd in a cold quicksilver sweat wilt lye
> A veryer ghost than I;

The laconic tail-line is nearer throwing away the incidental life of the diction than emphasising it: it is the covering of 'quicksilver sweat' which makes her more of a ghost than the ghost itself. And right through this minatory apostrophe the diction is loading the situation as if casually with a whole rich web of implication and innuendo that takes the poem quite beyond mechanical or formal contrivance, if only by the subtlety of the life and motives it calls in.

The Funerall still more patently compounds a *cento* of stock motifs: the lover's death of his mistress's disdain, the emblematic interpretation of the token she has sent him, the lover's complete dependence on his mistress for life and being, the lover as love's martyr, the lover's revenge. But these are all made to cohere in a live dramatic impulse, instinct with individual human voice and character. How far the counters have become alive and meaningful in Donne's mind and imagination is evident in the oblique attack, that quietly emphatic warning to the unknown layer-out, which makes the poem the critical part of a last urgently scribbled message. At the least the effect is surprise and delight as the reader sees the drift; but it also convinces by its representation of a man thinking through an immediate crisis.

The use of the same property of the love-token in *The Relique* for the same, perhaps complimentary, effect of the delicate avowal of devoted but hopeless love, points the considerable leap of the imagination by

which we are carried to the situation scores of years after their deaths,
when the reopening of the lover's grave reveals a scrap of bone still
with the lock of the lady's fair hair tied round it; a single evocation, too,
which most arrestingly demonstrates unalterable fidelity. The remote-
ness of this opening from any likely approach to the token-motif again
makes a double recognition part of the delight of the invention—first
of the device itself, and then of the way the opening situation has been
logically made to introduce it. But the poem comes to coherent life
because the device has prompted Donne's imagination to the creating of
a plot which not only absorbs the petrarchan property into a vivid
action but carries the entire argument, whose substance is precisely the
series of wild speculations put into the mouth of the remote grave-
digger, and the correcting avowal these provoke. The premises
themselves are full of incidental life and innuendo, from a macabre
reminder of human transience and the nothingness of flesh in a casual
parenthesis, to urbane glances at the credulity of those who make relics
of casually discovered bones. But they take Donne by smoothly un-
obtrusive ingenuity to his culminating stroke, the proclamation of love's
miracles. And here love's miracles are nothing to do with the co-
existence of incompatible physical elements, fire with ice and the like, or
the lover's own singular state; the peroration celebrates an uniquely
realised possibility in love itself, a condition of more than local concern.
Overall, Donne's distinctive invention is an artifice which permits and
vivifies the movement from the love-token to the celebration of love's
miracles; but he has used both movement and device to define a special
relationship between a man and a woman.

What one sees always is a fertile originality of invention, in the
service of an understanding which is not just provocatively unconven-
tional, but radically critical of the commitments implied in the very act
of writing love-verse. The aggressive casualness of attack is purposeful:

> I long to talke with some old lovers ghost
> (*Loves Deitie*)

This humanising anti-formality is also a calculated obliqueness, to bring
in the exercise of a questioning of Cupid's deity. But as much by innuendo as by open show, it redirects that old play. One is thrown back
to the first, natural, state of the Golden Age, celebrated by Ovid
(*Metamorphoses*, i) in terms which Tasso had memorably rewoven into a

lament for the time when feelings were at their purest and the word
'love' meant reciprocal passion, not one-sided devotion as now:

O bella età de l'oro
(*Aminta*, i, ii)

Donne's poem like Tasso's is an appeal to unperverted nature against the
cramping artificiality of present codes. But quite unlike Tasso's, its end
is a sifting of the nature of love itself, a tendency which is implicit in the
sudden but meaning-packed opening.

Other openings more directly assault expectation. 'Busie old foole,
unruly Sunne' makes a brusque contrast with the reverence customarily
accorded to the symbol of order and deity, and with Petrarch's 'Almo
Sol. . . .'—'Life-giving Sun!' The poem itself, *The Sunne Rising*, is a genre
piece looking back to Ovid (*Amores*, i, xiii), an aube, or morning song
requesting the day to delay and cursing its approach; and its central conceit is an extension of the petrarchan hyperbole that the mistress sums up
in herself all the world's treasures and beauties. In one way Donne simply
stands these themes on their head with immense panache, as his explosive
opening announces he will. The ground of the assault on the industrious
sun is not that he has come too soon but that he is misdirecting his efforts.
It is more important to provide these lovers with sexual energy than to
illumine the earth; which is anyway an uneconomic labour, since the
lovers sum up the whole world in themselves. But this doesn't seem
arbitrary, or argued for the comedy of these superbly patronising in-
solences. At least it has truth to what people really do feel; and from the
initial diminishing of the sun to the climactic hyperbole, it implies a
consistent reversal of accepted persuasions which amounts to a revaluation of the world's activities:

She'is all States, and all Princes, I,
Nothing else is.
Princes doe but play us; . . .
(*The Sunne Rising*)

The notorious compasses in *A Valediction: forbidding mourning* derive
from emblematic usage, but they no more parrot convention than they
perform something wildly *outré*. Coming where it does in the poem the
figure hasn't only to illustrate a condition already understood; which is all
Guarini can contrive with it. It is the climax of a movement carried

overall in analogies and alternative emblems, whose force is firstly to argue that the best love has the quietest leavetakings, and then to show why. And that is attempted by a kind of definition, a review which in demonstrating that this quietness is entailed in the nature of the best love becomes *ex hypothesi* an account of their interrelationship in absence, offering analogies and alternatives as a way of pinning something down as well as of evaluating it. It amounts, in sum, to a clarifying of the nature of the love itself. What is singular about the figure here is not at all that Donne applies it to two lovers, but the superior understanding it is made to reveal.

There is a care for the truth of events which subordinates reordering to weighed experience, and makes it purposeful. *The Good-morrow* offers a convincing representation of spontaneous mental life, but its essential content is a conceited play as intricately specious, in one sense, as any extravagance of courtly hyperbole. There is evident virtuosity in the construction of an organically evolving argument out of such a bizarre congeries of common elements—conceits developed as though they were literally true, emblematic properties and postures juggled-with to yield an extravagantly hyperbolic 'comparison from the less', a scrap of pseudo-medical lore made by chop-logic to prove an impossible proposition. But the true distinction of the feat is that its outcome is not trivial. Like the *Vita Nuova*, whose title-metaphor it domesticates, the poem plots the evolution of love from infantile unawareness to mature consciousness, and shows where the difference lies. And to make this discrimination is to determine what their love means to the lovers, how it stands in relation to the rest of secular experience, what is its essential condition of continuance. Quite literally, it is to show what Donne's understanding of love really amounts to.

2. *Movement*

The character of such lyric poems as *A nocturnall upon S. Lucies day*, *The Dissolution*, *Witchcraft by a picture*, differs sharply from Romantic models. The poem evokes and purports to dispose of a situation in real life; but the most obvious feature of it is that it doesn't develop by directly recounting an event, nor does the actual content of the poem amount to a plausible transcript of private experience. Overtly at any rate, content and development show a different concern. Seemingly, it is the working out of an intricate action or dialectical movement, in a brisk play which by its brilliance in its own right must have absorbed the poet's attention:

> On a round ball
> A workeman that hath copies by, can lay
> An Europe, Afrique, and an Asia,
> And quickly make that, which was nothing, *All*,
>> So doth each teare,
>> Which thee doth weare,
> A globe, yea world by that impression grow,
> Till thy teares mixt with mine doe overflow
> This world, by waters sent from thee, my heaven dissolved so.
>> (*A Valediction: of weeping*)

More deviously or less, this is the mode of the *Songs and Sonets*. The structure of the poem is just the disposition of the play as it evolves, a play sometimes remote in its actual terms from the situation itself, and sometimes directly reworking its circumstances, but always manifesting a consistent logic, its own intricate and possibly specious virtuosity.

This life of the poem is not extraneous to the circumstances from which it grows. The situation develops as through an extended metaphor, by an adroit coincidence between the autonomous life of the play and the sense at issue; the logical or anecdotal consistency of the play is the consistent meaningfulness, and completion, of the statement:

> My face in thine eye, thine in mine appeares,
> And true plaine hearts doe in the faces rest,
> Where can we finde two better hemispheares
> Witout sharpe North, without declining West?
>> (*The Good-morrow*)

To characterise the movement of a love poem as chop-logic or figurative dexterities is to seem to denote something inherently flippant. If this does not hold of the *Songs and Sonets* it is partly because the astonishing involutions rarely present themselves as a clever game. They are given the warrant of a dramatic circumstance which has all the appearance of warm actuality. The situation is made, often with complete naturalness and inevitability, to yield the play; and the commerce between the two is constantly felt to be live and meaningful. It is the acuity which controls this meaningfulness, as well as the more obvious adroitness, that is at issue when Donne's is termed a witty poetry.

Much of the movement of these lyrics is argumentative and involves close reasoning. One reason for this is the frequent casting of the whole poem in a disputative form. A claim is made which demands demonstration, a challenge offered which needs justifying or carries an implicit undertaking to make it good; something is professed which defies common probability, or logic, or the recognised pieties, but in any case brusquely reverses an expected stance. Often a gesture patently signals a *tour de force*. The claim is stepped up to an unsurpassable extreme as the movement progresses; a notorious theme proposed, offering rivalry with celebrated European handlings; a series of voluntaries invited, to make good some such unpromising proposition as that the lover's name scratched in a window will keep his mistress steady through a succession of likely temptations in his absence, or that the book of their love-letters comprises the entire body of civilised wisdom, and affords correctives for each profession.

This habitual address produces a distinctive character. There is a simulacrum of proof or legal pleading which requires the ingenious deployment of the formal processes of logic and rhetoric, and the management of the correlations between the properties of things basic to those disciplines:

> Were I a man, that I were one,
>   I needs must know; I should preferre,
>   If I were any beast,
> Some ends, some means; Yea plants, yea stone detest,
> And love; All, all some properties invest;
>   If I an ordinary nothing were,
> As shadow, a light, and body must be here.
>   (*A nocturnall upon S. Lucies day*)

Often enough a device is hardly felt as formal proof at all, but as conceited comparison or analogy, and even that may be assimilated into the living situation and made to subserve the rhetoric of the poem. The final stanza of *A Feaver* is essentially a last analogical application of the motif, which could have been handled mechanically, and weakly:

'The fever rages in you for a short time and then leaves you; so I would possess you devouringly even if my right in you should be brief.' In humanising this Donne has tightened it all ways:

> Yet t'was of my minde, seising thee,
>   Though it in thee cannot persever.
> For I had rather owner bee
>   Of thee one houre, then all else ever.

The slight personification of the fever—'seising thee'—makes it an exact, and therefore more meaningful analogue, and leads straight on to the last fervent affirmation.

For other purposes the logic is quite explicit, and even syllogistic in its formality. *The Dissolution* offers a quite egregious claim in demonstration of the unapproachable extremeness of the lover's reaction to his mistress's death: that the immoderateness of his grief will so explosively bring about his own death that his violently expelled soul will overtake hers in its flight. But the proof has the sober reasonableness of strict cause and effect. Materialisation of the common properties and final effects of extreme grief permits the compounding of these to form an explosive charge, the augmentation of grief being made to produce the augmentation of the combustion or explosion, and so vindicate the claim with the precision of a Q.E.D.

Commonly there is the appearance of inquiries more disinterestedly analytic. Something is to be probed, sifted, discovered, by the formal process of definition or classification. The three stanzas of *The Prohibition* offer the clash of directly contrary recommendations, and then a synthesis of these, a movement which justifies its paradoxical warnings and its reconciling of opposites by the promise of a subtler analysis of the motives of love than is usually made. In *The Primrose* it is a matter of sifting the several possibilities offered by the numerous flowers that surround him, and seeing that in rejecting either extreme he is forced back to the natural number of petals; a process whose emblematic import thus demonstrates to him that he must put up with mere peccant woman as she is, since either alternative is so monstrous. The centre of the dialectical process is a consideration of woman's nature as mistress, and the final 'answer', or vindication of the paradoxical clash of opposites is a resolved statement about that.

The movement of *Loves growth* presents a more orthodox rhetorical mode. Here it is a matter of finding ways of elucidating an apparent paradox of love, posed by the relativity of a lover's vows—a justification attempted by means of a metaphysical distinction and then a series of analogies and examples from cosmology, polity, and the like. The design is overtly explicatory, in that it is directed to showing analogically how an apparent contradiction is valid, but its effect is to move towards an understanding of the nature of a mature love through the rejection of inadequate accounts. Much of Donne's most striking imagery has this character of analysis or precise delineation. The difficulty posed by the initial stance or the movement of the argument becomes a search for the cipher which exactly discriminates a condition, pins down some critical deprivation, fixes a relationship; a formula which as often as not will carry the quiet endorsement of the metaphysical model on which it is constructed:

> Wee are
> The intelligences, they the sphaere.
> (*The Extasie*)

The manifest ingenuity on which such processes regularly depend elsewhere runs to a bravura manner of chop-logic, where the patent speciousness of the reasoning seems to be the first consideration. Extravagant quibbles and casuistries, often in support of some indefensible proposition, are the sinew of dialectical contortions whose immediate end appears to be to exceed probability or defeat expectation. In *Communitie* there is an exuberant remorselessness in summoning the arguments and distinctions which yield the proof of a quite outrageous position, a stroke capped by a still more outrageous analogy that demonstrates its point, but then is surprisingly and very succinctly made to yield another and shocking one:

> And when hee hath the kernell eate,
> Who doth not fling away the shell?

The violence to sense is pointed up by the very reasonableness of the logical design, the cool process of moral distinction and formal demonstration that women fall into the class of morally neutral things. In *Womans constancy* the wit lies as much as anything in the cumulative extravagance of the shifts by which the woman will seek to evade the implicit contract of their one-day relationship. Arguments starting as relatively sober legal quibbles work up in ever wilder improbability

through specious analogy to a deadly searching piece of chop-logic,
before the offhand reversal:

> Or, your owne end to Justifie,
> For having purpos'd change, and falsehood; you
> Can have no way but falsehood to be true?
> Vaine lunatique, against these scapes I could
> Dispute, and conquer, if I would,
> Which I abstaine to doe,
> For by to morrow, I may thinke so too.

These dialectical excesses parallel the more orthodox extravagance of
figurative dexterity, which is likewise constant in these poems. It is a
typical play to take literally the lament that the mistress's absence is an
eternity, and compute in meticulous detail the exact number of years or
centuries spent in the performance of each minute motion of longing.
The mode calls for hyperbolic claims, conceited manipulation of the
properties of figures, materialisations based on the shift of working out
literally the common figurative forms. Hearts literally contain pictures;
lovers physically intermingle as one being; tears, hearts, and eyes have
appropriate physical capacities, producing vast effects in the external
world. Donne, like petrarchan poets, regularly works these properties
up in small incidental actions:

> For thy face coines them and thy stampe they beare,
> And by this Mintage they are something worth,
> > (*A Valediction: of weeping*)

Sometimes he strings them together ingeniously to make up the plot of
an entire poem; as *Witchcraft by a picture*, which turns on whether his
image burns in her eye, drowns in her tear, or is safe in her heart, an
inquiry which thus sets up its own kind of dialectic and tension.

Here the typical lust to reach the inimitable extreme, to bring off an
unapproachable feat, is often undisguised. *A Feaver* makes the mistress's
sickness the fire which will burn the world, and asserts that she is a
paradigm or archetype of virtue and vital power who will take all these
from the world if she dies, leaving only ghosts and corrupt worms. *A
nocturnall upon S. Lucies day* typically humanises its conceited dialectics in
a vast 'comparison from the greater', which makes the devitalised
December world a model of life and gaiety compared to the bereaved
lover. He is systematically shown to be reduced by his mistress's death to

something lower than animal, vegetable, and mineral life, then to nothing, and less than nothing, and finally to the quintessence of nothing; a closely reasoned demonstration which is in fact the substance of the poem.

The appearance of a strict procedural logic points the artificiality of the way it is done:

> For if the sinewie thread my braine lets fall
> > Through every part,
> Can tye those parts, and make mee one of all;
> These haires which upward grew, and strength and art
> > Have from a better braine,
> Can better do'it;
>
> > > > *(The Funeral)*

This is a formal process (*ponendo ponens*) which argues the conceited proposition that the lock of her hair will be the means of preserving his body from dissolution in the grave. Its logical force rests in the identity made between the skein of sinews descending from the brain, which hold the body together, and the hair, also taken as growing from the brain. This identity is exploited in the form of an emblematic 'comparison from the less': the hair will be more effective even than the sinews, firstly because it comes from a better brain, and then because it grows upwards not downwards—it ascends (like the saved), not descends (like the corruptible). It is a mode which turns on the discovery of apt analogies, and the adroit establishment of correspondences or identities; and these commonly blazon their speciousness, founded as they are in accidental or contrived coincidences of properties, ingeniously exploited.

The ingenious process of establishing identities by meaningful coincidence of properties is central in Donne's poetry; as it is in Renaissance iconography, and in any intellectual discipline founded in a qualitative understanding of matter. It makes viable the brilliances by which he astonishes; and it makes these the language through which he communicates. It takes a diverting variety of modes. The 'device' of *A Valediction: of the booke* demands the presentation of the accepted attributes of love so as to offer correspondences with accepted aspects of the behaviour of the several professions. Hence the poem moves through a series of conceited identities established in as many particulars as possible—love and divinity, love and law, love and statecraft; and these yield the running possibility of reflecting satirically both ways at once, on love or the behaviour of lovers, and on the analogues them-selves. The series of very extravagant voluntaries in *A Valediction: of my name, in the window* turns on the ingenious interpretation of some dozen properties of the given motif, to make each of them yield some quality, motive, or lesson appropriate to the dramatic situation and the claim the poet has offered to demonstrate. A clever and delicate mani-pulation of correspondences is brought alive and given point and force by its natural assimilation to a dramatic action, and by the exuberant *brio* of the whole invention. In *The Will* again it is a matter of finding coincidences between the various vicious lessons the poet has learned in a long sufferance of the ways of love, and the perverse principles on which one might make bequests in a will; an invention whose power of double-edged satire is sharpened to the limit in a pattern which affords the virtuoso bite of continual unexpectedness.

The formal Paradox, understood as the witty justification of some such seemingly indefensible proposition as that it is better to have a sterile wife than a fecund one, had a European vogue in the sixteenth century and achieved its fashion in England at the time Donne was starting to write. But its presence in these poems signals more than an intellectual libertinism, whose one aim is to be as fantastically clever as possible while flouting every piety. The reversal of the accepted or anticipated position is frequently a means to a better understanding, or a searchingly different account of experience; avowedly so in *The undertaking*, where it is the gravamen of the poet's claim to heroism that the condition he delineates is an absurdity by conventional judgments, and unintelligible to conventional understandings.

The idea of a finely judged dramatic propriety may be more useful than a preoccupation with the sophistry of these intellectual gymnastics. Even the wildest logic chopping is not random. There is a sense of decorum at work, whose adjustments of tone quietly signal with what degree of seriousness one is to take a flourish, and a motivation which makes extravagances purposeful. In *A Jeat Ring sent* and *Sonnet. The Token*, the conjectured reasons for the gift are explicitly put forward as idle fancies, which any sensible man may discount at once in favour of a more down to earth explanation. In the same way, the dramatic point of the quibbling escapes and excuses in *Womans constancy* and *Lovers infiniteness* is precisely their egregiousness, pointing a gap between unacknowledged wish and attempted rationalisation which ought as

c

patently to signal motive as Leander's sophistries in the first sestiad of Marlowe's poem.

This motivating power can be delicate. The reversal which concludes *Womans constancy* turns on the abrupt and wholesale concession of all the possible evasions, in full recognition of their absurd speciousness, because they suit the poet's end too; the very casualness pointing the admission of such postcoital indifference as a likely motive in these relationships, too basic to need or bear rational explanation. In *Lovers infiniteness* the admitted insubstantiality of the mistress's conjectured escapes nicely discriminates the lover's state of mind, his timorous fumbling for a measure of self-confidence and certainty. These are giveaway absurdities often put into the mouths of other people. *The Relique* turns its pungent dramatic circumstance to the elaboration of some hopeful conjectures on the meaning of the lover's hair-encircled bone, where there is a double irony in the reader's recognising through these unrealities the characteristic softheadedness of people who might take a lover's bones for saints' relics, and at the same time, the justice of their doing so here in a sense they don't suspect and would deem blasphemous.

By the side of the conceited extravagances of late fifteenth century petrarchans, Donne's handling of the common language of figures and emblems seems impressively responsible. The typical petrarchan materialisations are made to signal the foolishness of others:

> What merchants ships have my sighs drown'd?
> Who saies my teares have overflow'd his ground?
> *(The Canonization)*

The actions constructed out of stock properties in *The Legacie, The Message,* and their like are at least consistently pertinent; and the title-figure in *The broken heart,* for one, embodies a pungent way of putting a traditional crux which conveys by the very adroitness of the application a warming sense of truth to what people really feel. Indeed there is a richer meaningfulness, which is continually apt to give life to seemingly quite neutral elements of diction—'curious traitors, sleavesilke flies/ Bewitch poore fishes wandring eyes'—and point to what would otherwise be preposterous figurative excesses. The lovers' hands are literally glued together, their eyes threaded on a double string, their souls go out leaving their bodies behind, and become one superior soul. Or their hearts are in their faces, which their eyes carry, and each reflection there shows them a hemisphere of a world superior to the larger world in that it remedies the geographical and climatic deficiences of that. Such intricacies take on precise emblematic value, and central relevance, as a way of dramatically embodying a sense going forward through the conceited play.

A less acceptable cleverness is that at work in a number of poems where the extravagance of the witty claim and its conceited justification is offered as a correlative of the immoderateness of the lover's feeling. Seeming to be indulged for its own sake, the play assumes an independent life and interest, and ultimately calls in question the whole relationship of tenor to vehicle on which Donne's lyric method depends. In *The Dissolution*, and *A Feaver*, as up to a point in *A nocturnall upon S. Lucies day*, the evident determination to bring off an unapproachable *tour de force*, or reach the unsurpassable limit of conceited invention, persuades the reader that ingenuity is the prior end and dissipates any sense of an immediate grief. What reality there may be has to be read back into a self-subsistent system kept in play by a compelling virtuosity, and in any case sometimes seems manipulated, as in *A Feaver*, to allow the poet to get the witty best of opposite possibilities, or as in *A Valediction: of weeping* merely the expected 'given', to show his cleverness in doing new things with it.

The difficulty here is partly the artificiality of a convention that calls for the working out of an elaborate analysis of grief in a way apparently remote from the reality of feeling. It is also a danger of the method itself, which always invites a feat of double horsemanship. Yet this virtuosity too can be a positive artistic force. The conspicuous success of poems like *The Good-morrow* and *Aire and Angels* rests in their simultaneous evolving of intricate play and subtly discriminated meaning, so that every exhilarating advance of one is a richer exploration or finer nuance of the other. In *Aire and Angels* the self-catechism carried in the developing figure is not only sharp as a proving of the true nature of love, and an implied criticism of petrarchan attitudes, but close enough to the reality of experience to give one a sense of warm insight as the play develops. The interest here is at least equal to one's interest in the development of an intricate play of conceit from a stock motif. Or more accurately, in this poem these are the same interest.

3. Form

Donne's longstanding reputation for roughness seems questionable if it carries the imputation of formal crudity. Such poems as *The Prohibition, The Blossome, The Dampe*, show an uncommon concern with pattern and a quite unprecedented skill in its assimilation to dialectical ends; a mastery which Donne flamboyantly advertises in the kind of rhapsody-on-one-note virtuosity with which he circles round 'all' in *Lovers infiniteness*, or 'love' in *The Canonization*. And this is far from mere verbal chiming. It is a sophistication of the formal effect essayed rather artlessly by Wyatt, in which the recurrence of the pattern is not only given strict point and relevance but a subtly fresh direction each time, so that the effect is of great difference within apparent sameness. Wyatt's *Deem as ye list*, say, makes an interesting comparison with the wonderfully adroit and insistent movement of *Loves Deitie*, whose schematic repetitions, fixed by the recurrent swirling round the key line, are in fact the mainspring of the dialectical movement, tensing the series of lithe twists which are the life of the poem. This is a manner taken to the limit of virtuosity in *The Will*, a thoroughly schematic poem which precisely exploits the effect of a recurrent pattern, regular expectation, by offering a succession of different applications of a like formula, a new and pungent twist to go on evading expectation long after you had thought he couldn't possibly contrive it yet again.

There seems a care for formal decorum which seeks exact appropriateness in the use of a stanza form. This goes much beyond the opportunist effects evident everywhere—the jaunty riding movement in *Song*, 'Goe, and catche', the innumerable exploitations of the irregularity of the stanza pattern for point or weight. It amounts to a delicate sense of fitness, which puts Donne's immense rhetorical resource in the service of dramatic and dialectical ends. It is not chance that pieces as differently motivated as *A Valediction: forbidding mourning* and *A Feaver* are so appropriately accommodated in an identical stanza form. In *A Valediction: forbidding mourning* the simplicity and quietness of the fall of the brief stanza, and the steady pulsing movement, overriding any momentary jar, make the poem a series of muted and self-contained utterances, almost laconic in their extreme clipped simplicity; a character which is dramatically right and indeed part of the sense of the poem. Whereas *A Feaver* opens at once with a rhetorical outburst which breaks right across the line-scheme to unfold a long logic-chopping hyperbole. The determining consideration seems to be the kind of play Donne chose to make of either possibility, which demanded in both cases a predominance of short pungent statements complete within the stanza, or at most balancing one stanza against the next.

This organic utilisation of form marks out *A Valediction: of weeping*. Here Donne's ability to treat an idea like a dramatic plot, holding it over a whole stanza to a final resolution, serves several quite different ends. In the first stanza, as the last, it is the means by which the force of the initial outburst is maintained and the sense made to flow through in a rhetorical pattern which seems the shape of the emotion itself. The long cries, broken by staccato exclamations, sweep one on to the concluding four-teener whose extra length is used for the complete articulation of an intricate resolving idea. Yet in stanza 2 the same pattern at once convincingly lends itself to something more like riddling, the sense unwinding intricately through the oblique play of analogy and emblematic application to a hyperbolic claim which is only fully clinched in the very last words. Idea is again perfectly assimilated to form, the structure of the stanza seeming the organic embodiment of the complex thought. This is a subtle congruence which goes down to intimate particulars:

> So doth each teare
> Which thee doth weare,
> A globe, yea world by that impression grow,

The delaying of the verb holds the statement taut, and the 'globe, yea world', so naturally slipped in as spontaneous revision, is a rhetorical shift which actually clinches the emblem-play. Dramatic rhetoric and conceited play are also completely at one.

Some of Donne's finest pieces are extremely sophisticated formal structures, whose power lies partly or mainly in the artistry of their rhetorical patterning. *The Anniversarie* gets much of its excitement from Donne's intimate exploitation of the peculiarities of a very irregular stanza-form, which he still further diversifies by internal variation in phrase-length. Its rhetorical skill lies in the way the cumulative schematic patterns are piled up by delayed resolution on to the single emphatically short line, to pick out the point like the sudden sharp announcement of a leitmotive, before the grand march starts up again, with its repetitions and half-repetitions pounding out the proclamation to the final perorative trumpet shout in the last line. The nice articulation of these final announcements shows how succintly form and meaning, oratory and dialectics, are made one in this poem, down to the exact exploitation of the extra foot in the alexandrine:

> But truly keepes his first, last, everlasting day.

One gets a movement of hammering vehemence, whose effect is to point the paradoxical truth very deliberately and starkly, then to seem to snatch it up for the final triumphant triple-stressed blast.

In another rhetorical 'tour de force', *A nocturnall upon S. Lucies day*, the constant repetitions of the verbal and schematic pattern set up a kind of tolling—'yeares . . . dayes . . . Lucies'; and the effect is sustained over eight lines of lugubriously resonant pondering of the single irreducible point, which pursue the awful consequences further and further down, to the absolute extremity:

> shrunke,
> Dead and enterr'd;

The short lines, far from weakening the gait, have a most telling finality, a sense of the brief lapidary announcement of universal desiccation:

> The worlds whole sap is sunke:

Formal pattern and rhetorical scheme here have very much the effect of pointing. 'Were I a man, that I were one,/I needs must know; I should preferre,/*If I were any beast,*/ Some ends, some means;'—the sudden extra-emphatic rising line is slipped in to say with far greater and pithier vehemence that he is not even a beast. And throughout, this enormously subtle phrasing artfully diversifies the pattern of the stanza to build the overall rhetorical movement whose irresistible stride makes this such a magnificent piece.

Donne's concern with patterning doesn't bind him to the formal pattern of the stanza; and it is both the violence and the persistence of his disruptions of his elected stanza forms that single him out. In these poems even a simple effect like enjambement is likely to produce a radical dislocation of sense and syntax together, in which coupled parts of speech are sundered, and possibly held apart over several lines by the intervention of a parenthesis; a colossal syntactical stammer, as it appears.

But this is a positive feature of poems like *The Blossome* and *A Lecture upon the Shadow*, whose essence is a studied casualness of tone and movement:

> Disguises did, and shadowes, flow,
> From us, and our cares; but, now 'tis not so.

The power of the run-on to set up a pattern of suspense and climax makes it a favoured instrument of a poet who constantly manipulates syntax to draw one on to a crucial emphasis, or a resolution. The last five lines of *Loves Deitie* show a consummately wicked use of the formal pattern for something like an oratorical purpose, compelling one to read the stanza in the way which affords the greatest possible bite; an effect of a promised *coup* repeatedly held off, before the cogs suddenly mesh and the screw is turned, bit by bit:

> Yet shee
> Will bee
> False, ere I come, to two, or three.
> (*Song*, 'Goe, and catche')

Such shifts are as integral to Donne's particular mode of poetic statement as sensuous imagery is to Keats's. It is the character of his rhetoric to point up the natural emphasis of the speaking voice:

> . . . what thou, and I
> Did, till we lov'd?
> (*The Good-morrow*)

—or positively to explode his meaning in one's face:

> it could not chuse but bee
> Prophane, to thinke thee any thing but thee.
> (*The Dreame*)

Or he exploits the pause to get one reaching for the sense, at times the wrong sense, thus setting up a false expectation which barbs the resolution when it comes:

> Kill mee as Woman, let mee die
> As a meere man;
> (*The Dampe*)

In particular, this is the means of his most characteristic stroke of the quick throwaway line, the sudden twist, the slight deadpan aside which is the more destructive because it seems at first to say nothing much:

> thinke that yet
> We'had never met.
> (*Loves Usury*)

At times these dislocations approach barbarousness. There seems a wanton disregard of normal consideration in *The Legacie*, where we are dragged into a long ramifying parenthesis after only four words, and thus held from the main sense until the fifth line of the poem. A brutal complication of syntax toughens *A Valediction: of my name, in the window*, whose odd little stanza pattern is all but burst apart with the constant straining of the most perverse parentheses, inversions, clause-structures, rammed forcibly into it to give a feeling of extreme muscular contortedness; an aggressive intractibility which the poem has in common with such other grittily low-life pieces as *The Curse* and *The Will*. The pursuit of expository fluidity sometimes lures Donne to a looseness which doesn't seem far from prose; though the experiment of actually writing out in prose such an extreme example as stanza 2 of *Loves growth* shows even here a good deal more schematic artifice than appears. Or one gets a dislocation so extreme as to risk formal collapse. In the middle section of *Farewell to love* the feel of the form is lost, and the character of the pattern apparently disregarded; there is something that looks like disdainful casualness in the way the short lines are used to carry purely mechanical parts of the statement.

Yet one's impression is rarely of an arbitrary unorthodoxy. The irregularity of *The Apparition*, where the apostrophe sweeps in a continuous flow through seventeen lines of haphazardly varied length, gives a vivid impression of thought developing just in that way—growing, shrinking, pausing, quickly seizing on something or tossing it away, throwing up parentheses and epithets which the long lines absorb with seeming inevitableness; an irregularity, even so, held in felt pattern round the simple rhyme scheme. The mobile phrasing of *The Dampe*, shaped by the tight formal pattern, sweeps one on with it and very much gives the impression of an intricate idea evolving there and then; the loose syntax seeming to be infinitely extensible, and quite spontaneously growing as fresh notions or aspects occur to the lover. The apparently unrehearsed and haphazard movement of casual speech seems to be the effect of decidedly artful manipulations of syntax. In *The Flea* there is a continual sense of things added as if suddenly thought of, of new emphasis and then still further emphasis:

Where wee almost, yea more than maryed are.

                                    . . . this
    Our mariage bed, and mariage temple is;

The withholding of the verb and the self-correcting addition points up
and clinches a central play, under an exact simulacrum of spontaneous
speech.

    This is an artifice which feeds the essential life of such poems as *Loves
Usury:*

        Till then, Love, let my body raigne, and let
        Mee travell, sojourne, snatch, plot, have, forget,
        Resume my last yeares relict:

The heavy stress on the unresolved neutral verb 'let', a consequence of its
harsh separation from its object, makes emphatic the fact of a fresh
demand; but it also gives the impression of something just occurring to
him, which makes him add this so forcibly and then hold things up while
he gets it clear before speaking. The line following is a real *tour de force*,
with its effect of things being spontaneously added; more and more
enormities, each word a little explosive charge at which you have to
pause, and think, and adjust yourself afresh. Here too the pattern itself,
finely handled, helps to suggest tone and mood as well. Something is
suddenly seen or arrived at, which gives him a jaunty self-satisfaction:

                This bargaine's good;

—the mid-line arrest, with the consequent heavy stress on 'good',
compelling one to read it with rising inflection, and communicating
precisely the mood of the utterance. Throughout this poem in fact, the
very fluid phrasing and intricate syntactical pattern not only catch most
delicately a precise shade of dramatic tone and emphasis, but suggest a
kind of gay spontaneity—things added unrehearsed with accelerating
verve and abandon, invention kindling, and warming to greater and
greater comic excesses.

    Nor indeed does the movement itself usually feel formless; on the
contrary, in extreme fluidity one has a strong sense of pattern:

            His office was indulgently to fit
        Actives to passives. Correspondencie
        Only his subject was; It cannot bee
        Love, till I love her, that loves mee.
                                (*Loves Deitie*)

The arrangement of the phrases sets up what amounts to a counter-pattern, but the feel of the formal pattern is not lost; it is held firm by the emphatic rhyme-words and the rhythm of the whole movement. So there is a kind of formal counterpointing; the regular pattern of the stanza is made to pull against a different pattern set up by the phrasing, and both elements are constantly felt together:

> that I who still was true,
> In life, in my last Will should cozen you.
> (*The Legacie*)

The intricate schematic arrangement gives maximum point to the ironic oppositions—'I . . . you', 'true . . . cozen', 'life . . . my last Will'.

This seems to be an instrument of considerable expressive subtlety, as well as dramatic emphasis, often indeed where phrasing seems loosest:

> Deare love, for nothing lesse than thee
> Would I have broke this happy dreame,
> It was a theame
> For reason, much too strong for phantasie,
> (*The Dreame*)

The shifting syntactical pattern tugs against the formal pattern to pick out the crucial 'thee', and to balance 'reason' against 'phantasie', pulling the voice round to the right expressive emphasis. And there are more critical functions:

> But wee will have a way more liberall,
> Than changing hearts, to joyne them so wee shall
> Be one, and one anothers All.
> (*Lovers infinitenesse*)

Phrasing, verbal scheme, and speech-rhythm make up a pattern which cuts across the formal pattern and rhyme-scheme without submerging them; and the tensions thus set up afford a system of articulation delicate in the extreme. The least regular pieces show very close attention to this:

> Since so, my minde
> Shall not desire what no man else can finde,

The entire ten lines of this final stanza of *Farewell to love* show a consummate rhetorical artifice. Every formal element—rhyme, rhythm, stress, line-length, formal pattern—is utilised to articulate the structure of the idea itself. Terms are counterpoised, points linked or paralleled, oppositions pointed, key words and images picked out.

Here is a rhetoric so subtly artful that it makes the formal scheme one element in the whole apparatus of articulation and pointing; a radical way of widening the possibilities of schematic expression. These complex patterns and intertensions are constantly working in the *Songs and Sonets*, felt but not obtrusive:

> Let me not know that others know
> That she knowes my paines, least that so
> A tender shame make me mine owne new woe.
> (*Loves exchange*)

> As the first were made to blinde
> Others; these which come behinde
> Will worke upon our selves, and blind our eyes.
> (*A Lecture upon the Shadow*)

There is a deliberate breaking down of the set stanza pattern, but the imposition too of a system of tight controls across the freer movement, which not only keeps the statement in pointed order, but always lets one feel the formal regularity behind the new pattern set up, and in fact uses the element of formal shape to build the new pattern.

This sophisticated rhetoric is the necessary instrument of Donne's complex poetic statement. It gives him the flexibleness of prose with a pungency, and pointed articulation, beyond prose; and it immediately enacts an intricate interconnectedness rare in any art. Absolute control of formal syntax enables him to organise a great variety of statement structures; and in particular to break up the regular pattern almost indefinitely, in any number of syntactical complications, without losing the feel of the form. He can keep more or less to the formal units, or set up a variety of syntactical units of his own within or across them. And there is an intimate regulation of speed and emphasis, for he has the possibility of stopping to stress every word, if he wants to, or of working-in the most intricate dependencies or qualifications. It is the possibility of a variety of flexible small units that makes these much qualified, richly stuffed movements possible; as it is management of syntax that makes the form or pattern seem the inevitable structure of the complex idea itself. Donne can assimilate almost any idea to any form, because he can so intimately control its development.

Donne's rhythmic disturbances are likewise not casual carelessness, but central to his poetic mode and character. Here too there is a kind of decorum at work, in the appropriateness of regularity or of liberty to the kind of thing he is saying and the way he is saying it. More specifically, Donne's rhythms represent a variety of attempts to exploit the pull between regularity and fluidity, formal metre and the rhythms of natural speech. The imposing of a kind of counterstressing against the mechanical beat of the formal metre serves the counter-patterning, as in most of the examples given. But this counterstressing is basic to the simultaneous effort to point, and to heighten dramatic verisimilitude with the accent of the living voice; two intentions which can themselves be at odds. Here too the minimum aim is a controlled naturalness, the feel of regularity under seeming freedom:

> Weepe me not dead, in thine armes,

> To make dreames truths; and fables histories;
> Enter these armes,

> Sunke so low, as to love one which did scorne.

The vehement speech-accent imposes a strong stress on a syllable formally weak; or a stress-pattern is violently inverted; or the formal accent imposes a heavy stress on a neutral word which would go unstressed or unremarkably accented in normal English speech.

To get the effects such irregularities give, Donne seems ready to risk much, perhaps too much; and certainly to rely heavily on the reader's co-operation. There are places in the *Songs and Sonets* where a reading with the natural speech-rhythm won't scan, but a reading according to the strict formal metre yields vivid pointing or emphasis:

> That she knowes my paines,

The mechanical stressing of the formal metre fetches up quite unnaturally, but hence with violent emphasis, the antithesis of 'she . . . my'. Or again—

> Onely let mee love none, no, not the sport;

To read this as the pentameter the other stanzas show it should be, one has to stress and phrase it in a way which compels a particular tone of voice and emphasis—a vehement fervour which throws one from 'Onely' to 'none', enforces the pause, and then sweeps one up to the still more vehement climax on 'sport'. Dramatic emphasis, the feel of the man uttering it with live point, is preferred to immediate clarity of rhythm.

But this is chancy. There are as many instances where the price of some vehemence is the loss of the feel of the formal metre, though that may be exactly observed as it almost always is; or where counterpointing is so radical that the speech-accent pulls the statement towards a free prose rhythm, or rhythmic anarchy:

> Study me then, you who shall lovers bee
> At the next world, that is, at the next Spring:
> (*A nocturnall upon S. Lucies day*)

The consequence is a number of places where you have to look at other lines or stanzas to find what the metre is, and this perhaps at the start of a poem, before any norm has been established—'As virtuous men passe mildly away'. And the result still may not satisfy:

> Thou shalt be a Mary Magdalen, and I
> A something else thereby;
> (*The Relique*)

The longer line scans mechanically as the iambic pentameter the other stanzas have at this point. But if a reading with five heavy stresses seems idiosyncratic, no other makes sense.

Donne's rhetoric is tightrope walking, dependent on the tension maintained while one feels both norm and variant simultaneously, always risking collapse with the loss of the feel of the norm; and more dangerously so with metre, where we can only fumble for accents the poet himself took for granted. *Farewell to love*, possibly the toughest poem in the *Songs and Sonets*, is a deeply radical and at times hazardous exploration of formal possibilities, to the end of articulating a poetic argument of extreme complexity. The prodigious intellectual feat pivots on the movement of the third stanza, which attempts a simultaneous presentation of a complex of interconnected ideas quite bemusing in its intricacy, a mesh of qualification and dependency the syntax reflects. And it is all but indigestible. The sheer strain of getting it articulated at all issues in cryptic sense at the expense of all else: the syntax is too violently dislocated, the patterns run too strongly athwart, the movement divaricates shapelessly:

> Unless wise
> Nature decreed (since each such Act, they say,
> Diminisheth the length of life a day)
> This, as shee would man should despise
> The sport;

The reader, left unsupported, hangs giddily on the edge of chaos.
In all, Donne's formal idiosyncrasy is integral to his poetic character.
The great majority of the pieces in the *Songs and Sonets* are in irregular
stanzas, either single or repeated. But these are not complex in any
traditional mould. It is not a matter of a set arrangement of lines and an
intricate rhyme scheme, into which everything must fit, but a kind of
organic structure; the dominant element is less the feel of a constantly
repeating pattern and chime—for regularity may be felt only as a faint
ground bass—than a sense of controlled yet fluid growth. The pleasure is
not that of finding the new or unexpected accommodated to the
expected and predictable, but of feeling unexpected and perhaps only
half-realised correspondences and schemes in the midst of new and
seemingly free growth. There is pattern too, but one has the feeling at
least of a pattern growing straight out of the structure of the statement
itself; a style much nearer oratorical prose than, say, Tasso's, or Dow-
land's, where the swing of the recurrent formal movement sets up its
own necessity, and pleasure, and imposes on the material to the extent of
dictating the mode of statement. Donne uses his pattern—establishes it
and then varies it internally by the usual devices of phrasing and counterpointing; but the result is a freer plasticity, for the pattern itself is casual,
and the variations risk breaking it down altogether, running into the still
greater freedom of prose.

None the less the formal element is dominant in him. He makes
patterns with and across the stanza pattern, and he exploits them all the
time for some effect of tension, suspension, emphasis, turn, sharp
pointedness. In this he is to be contrasted with a later poet like Keats, in
whom a run-on is the continuance of a statement, or at most an intensi-
fication of it—'My heart aches, and a drowsy numbness pains/My sense'.
Donne's representative formal pattern is that of *The Dampe*, where the
movement set up in the evolving syntax is also evolving logic, modified as it goes, ramifying, but always taking one forward to grasp the
logical sequence or argument. In this Donne is with Milton, a rhetorical
poet, and a rhetorically trained and conscious one, calculatedly exploring
and exploiting the formal possibilities of English speech.

4. Love

1. The sport

The milieu of such poems as *The Curse*, *The Indifferent*, *Loves Usury*, *The Apparition*, *Loves diet*, is a cavalier one familiar from Renaissance low comedy. This is a young man's world, in which women are mere objects, to be tried, enjoyed, and lightheartedly discarded; and the worst indignity it offers is that which diminishes a man's self-sufficiency by reducing him to a humiliating slavery and so sapping his independence. Hence faithful love is unnatural, restrictive, an indignity of middle-age, and fidelity itself a heresy which had better be purged ruthlessly if a man is to enjoy his due prerogative of change, and his particular freedom to hawk unconcernedly at whom he pleases; or for that matter to devise seductions which at one stroke yield a double or triple pleasure by their witty effrontery:

> mistake by the way
> The maid, and tell the Lady of that delay;
> > (*Loves Usury*)

The woman-hunt is 'the sport'; and even that is not to be loved, lest it bring its own restriction of liberty. At best, love is a contract imposed by the exigencies of the chase, to be evaded by legal quibbling like any other contract. The mutual instability of any sexual relationship may be taken for granted; as may the ephemeralness of women's affections, and the palpable speciousness of the highflown principles they profess—mere special pleadings, excuses for change which one pretends to indulge only because it suits one's own purpose. Women, in sum, are frail beings in a world of exploiters, by nature loving 'diverse experience', and professing such principles as chastity and virginity purely for tactical advantage—which they won't hesitate to take, for money, or bodily pleasure, or mere perverseness. And this is not only a characterisation of woman; it is an estimation of the kind of world this is. Possibly there are somewhere spheres in which wives aren't 'cursed', don't betray a husband by yielding easily to his foes, don't deceive him over the parentage of children; but that is what one expects, and repeatedly finds here. Possibly in a less sophisticated environment beauty and faithfulness might co-exist in women; here you will never find a woman who is both, or if by some prodigious feat of remote discovery you should, she would not stay so for more than a moment in the exploiting ethos of our society.

The world thus represented may be conscienceless, but it would be quite untrue to the spirit of these poems to call it crude or animal; and mindless it certainly is not. Nor is the representation of it necessarily trivial. One responds to it for the positive qualities it has: the life, the gusto, the sense of a Rabelaisian relish for experience which expresses itself in this spirit of comic extravagance and hyperbole. This is a zest, indeed, which is so far from coarseness that it manifests itself in conduct in a marked elegance of style—a bland and jaunty insouciance, a gay self-reliance. Moreover, we are in the real world, even if it is a partial picture of it that we get. As a generalisation it would certainly be unfair; but as a generalisation, the world of idealised love would be untrue.

The ebullient self-sufficiency of, say, *The Indifferent*, is a world away from the courtly and petrarchan posture of abject servility, hopeless dependence on the caprice of a notoriously unstable sex. But if that is quite uncourtly, such pieces as *The Flea* and *The Dampe*, which by their petitionary form invite direct comparison, seem provocatively anti-courtly. It isn't only that both are persuasions to bodily pleasure, or that they belong to that Ovidean world in which women are skilled contestants, who have to be outflanked by rhetorical virtuosity before they are won. Far more deflationary of the high pretensions of the religion of love are the central devices, coolly announced in the titles. Donne uses a lovers' colloquy to carry the Berni-esque *jeu d'esprit* of a magnification of a trivial or sordid object;[1] an object moreover, in *The Flea*, which is made to intimate emblematically that it is not faithful service which is in view but the quite uncourtly end of marriage. And *The Dampe* is still more brazenly uncourtly. It pipes up the hallowed properties of *courtoisie*—disdain, honour, constancy, secrecy—simply to exorcise them brutally. This lover doesn't profess secrecy and constancy, or (seemingly) love either; the abatement of her disdain and honour leads not to his salvation but to his 'death'; the end of courtship is not

---

[1] The Florentine poet Francesco Berni (d. 1535) won himself European notoriety for his witty poems in praise of the plague, fleas, gluttons, being in debt, urinals and the like. The fashion derived from poems by Virgil and Ovid, on a gnat and a flea respectively.

one-sided devotion but the naked prosecution of love's war, on equal terms, in bed.

2. Rebel and atheist

A number of poems in the *Songs and Sonets* challenge closer comparison. Abstractly put, in fact, their plots seem to present a lover as abject as any petrarchan. He suffers pain from her refusal of his love, more pain from hearing his lament sung; he is broken hearted, dying, dead, of her hardheartedness or scorn; he laments or complains that his faithful love, which seeks only marriage with her, is cheapened by her lightness. Or he cries out on the capricious tyranny of Love himself, who has killed him by making him love where he cannot possibly get a return, and where the woman is insulted by his love; or whose usurpations have perverted the first primal state of nature in which love for love was the innate condition.

A very slight acquaintance with European petrarchism will show how much of its properties Donne takes for granted as the essential fabric of his poetry. Yet the feel is wholly unlike. This is partly because of the particular uses he makes of the properties he reworks. But much more, it is because of the very different style of his approach, which is always pulling even conventional materials round to point another way. The effect of the following out of a situation or a complex sense through a consistent witty action is not here to put a mere figurative gloss on the point, or to lose that altogether in the machinery of the play, but to imply a degree of detachment, a zest in the execution itself, and often in the world of affairs outside the personal fact, quite different from the inbred lugubriousness of courtly lament. The emblematic play in *A Jeat Ring sent*, with its cool appraisal of the properties and values of the token and unruffled teasing it out to the worst of its possible messages, carries its plain suggestion of the poet's uncommittedness more cogently than any explicit avowal; as it also quietly urges the uncourtly drift that the end of such a relationship is marriage. The whole movement of poems like *The Legacie* and *The Will* is cast to point a vivacity, a half-amused or sardonic zest in the articulation of the dialectical apparatus, that is quite at odds with any sense of the lover's over-commitment to his own misfortunes; the disclosure of which is anyway so placed that it is the quick stab of unexpected point that occupies one's mind.

Donne's attitude swings between sophisticated wariness and sceptical

D

detachment, and always presents itself as a refusal to make unguarded commitments. Unconsciously or by design this is just what the whole movement of several of these poems acts out. *Witchcraft by a picture* turns on a sceptical sense of the equivocalness of the usual tokens of sincere passion—tears, looks, sighs, and the rest—and the insistence that these be tested, albeit by another common touchstone, before acceptance. In *The Token* itself the conventional usage announced in the title, and then meticulously exhibited, is pointedly crumbled; the inquiry works its way to a positive assurance by the rejection, in a whole rhetorical scheme of negatives, of all the common coin. So that the implied evaluation is at once sophisticated and sceptical—'These are rather childish shifts after all; and what indeed can such shallow devices possibly tell you about the reality!' The request he does make in the face of the code is deceptively humble, but it gives the formula of the love-posie fresh point and direction:

> But swear thou thinkst I love thee, and no more.

Love-tokens are easy coin, Troilus's favour finishes up in Diomed's coat; but her sincere recognition of his love is a positive and an assured gain. The mode is to oppose a psychological insight to mechanical acceptances; the standard is modest but tested reality against large pretension.

Nor is this the central difference. That seems to lie less in Donne's view of other models of love than in his attitude to his own experience, and to himself. In *Loves Deitie* it isn't only the overt denial of the basis of courtly servitude in the assertion that an unreciprocated love is no love, or the turn in the last stanza, where the poet goes back on himself only to impale another article of the courtly code:

> Falshood is worse then hate; and that must bee,
> If shee whom I love, should love mee.

The critical distinction is the bland irony implicit alike in the casual earnestness of the approach and in the seeming acquiescence in the stock characterisation of love; the expostulatory modulations of tone carry a nice self-mockery:

> Rebell and Atheist too, why murmure I,

That is a piquancy one feels again in *Twicknam garden*, where the self-

dramatising postures of the 'Zefiro torna' theme,[1] and the rueful solem-
nity of the final denunciation, are made to sound their own exaggeratedness. The over-ceremonious gravity of manner, and such continual
deflating touches as the hard realism of the emblems he chooses, make the
poem a huge high-comic hyperbole:

> But O, selfe traytor, . . .
> O perverse sexe, . . .

Here, the tone assures us, is a man who is not likely to take his own
attitudinising too seriously, or his subject either. And this too is a poise
which, sometimes more explicitly sometimes less, is built into the movement of these poems. *The Triple Foole* turns on the poet's detached
attitude to himself, his ironic recognition of his own manifold foolishness; and it gets much of its bite from its belittlement of his own poetic
pretensions.

It is precisely this equivocal relation to his own impulsions which *The
Blossome* dramatises as the dialogue between the poet and his heart, a
debate significantly aligned to give all the advantage to the prescient
judgment. Detachment could go no further than the humouring indulgence the coolly appraising judgment extends to a heart ignorant even
of its own standing; but more telling than self-awareness is control. The
Astrophel of Sidney's sequence, like many another petrarchan, and
Petrarch himself, clearly recognises his grim plight but is powerless to
amend it while his heart rules his judgment; a poem like *The Blossome*
seems precisely cast to demonstrate the unmanliness of such deeply
committed subservience as that.

The calm reasonableness with which *The Funerall* chronicles the poet's
killing dependence on his mistress takes any harshness out of the final
turning of tables, which appears more as a last bravura gesture of attachment than as a revenge. Revenge indeed is hardly consonant with an
attitude which, like that of *The Blossome* and *Twicknam garden*, is nearer
simple human respect than reverence or hatred. Petrarch insures some of
his greatest successes with the sheer grandiloquence of his address. The
quite unexalted attack of Donne's love lyrics carries its own orientation:

> When I dyed last, and, Deare, I dye
> As often as from thee I goe,
> > (*The Legacie*)

[1] Petrarch's sonnet which opens with these words tells how the return of
spring has surrounded the lover with a reanimation that mocks him.

The conceit is petrarchan, but this certainly isn't genuflection before a semi-deity; in fact it is immediately recognisable as the note of common respect and tenderness. One needs to remind oneself that there are radically different levels of experience involved here, that Donne's manner would no more have been suitable to the hymning of transcendental truth than the tone of the *Divina Commedia* would fit domestic affection. If Donne doesn't domesticate, he humanises the emotion:

> My ragges of heart can like, wish, and adore,
> But after one such love, can love no more.
> (*The Broken heart*)

The old neo-mystical figure of the shattering impact of love, not so far from Dante's account for that matter, is made finally to convey a quite particularised feeling and a common human truth.

Such writing may not suggest transcendent elevation, but it rings true to life. It is the implicit assumption in *The Will* that the common human relationship is all that matters—a view so regularly taken for granted that one sometimes wonders if Donne could have had any real sense of what a transcendental love poetry, such as Michelangelo's, was about. The positive truth so carefully worked towards in *The Token* is an acute observation about people's motives, and in particular the way they act and react to one another. More strikingly in *Loves exchange*, if only because for once Donne does express the abjectness of the slave of love, the courtly formulary becomes a way of moving to a quite different order of experience. The poem puts, in the ingeniously vivid figure of a siege-won town, the classic case of the rebel against love who eventually succumbs the more abjectly; and it also contrives from the same figure a quite petrarchan compliment, suggested in a deft transference by which Love's conquering mien becomes the mistress's irresistible face. As so often in Donne the battery of sighs, tears, evasions and the like appear as the flimsy stock-in-trade of the professional lover, the woman-hunter; while the real lover is the hapless man who loves once, and hopelessly, feels the shame of his humiliation, and asks for death rather than the present torture. If an abstract summary still suggests some surface affinity with courtly servitude, the poem is in feeling and in focus a long way from the fiction of the lover groaning in secret under the strokes of the tyrant passion:

> Let me not know that others know
> That she knowes my paines, . . .

One is switched rudely from the mystique of ennobling devotion, the self-humbling implicit in such a relationship, to sole concern with the lover's sophisticated anguish over his own social vulnerability. By contrast, this seems to be very much a real man in the real world.

Words like sincerity, truth, reality are relative in their literary application and may have as much relevance to good courtly poetry as to Donne's. Neither order of experience can be disregarded. Donne's special truth relates to a field not much explored in post-classical poetry until his time; it lies in a finely discriminated fidelity to natural experience. What he pins down, that is to say, is not a moral insight or a final truth, or anything directly to do with the transcendental aspiration of the spirit at all; but something with the recognisable feel of common actuality. It is the report of the man who in mundane affairs has been there, and got inside the experience.

Nothing more forcibly illustrates the moral tendency of Petrarch's passion than his ultimate renunciation of love, a turn from the world, and dismissal of the things of the flesh, whose exaltation Sidney catches and if anything points up in his *Splendidis longum valedico nugis*—'Leave me o love, which reachest but to dust'. Donne too has his *Farewell to love*, whose mordant sombreness certainly doesn't argue flippancy. But if Petrarch's recantation, with Sidney's, marks a kind of ascetic platonism—a rising above transient flesh and mere appearance to a timeless traffic in the real world of the spirit—then Donne's is determinedly naturalistic and aristotelian. The love he dismisses is nothing so rigorous as a long and selfless martyrdom of devotion, but avowedly the woman-hunt; and the stand he takes is post-experience, and psychological. Here, just as in the *Canzoniere*, there is a final realisation after repeated disillusionment that secular love is always a cheat, a humiliation, a self-destroying frenzy; but this has nothing to do with hard-achieved moral maturity, that at last lets him see the sinfulness of years of false worship and turns him to the only valid love. Here too there is a moral absolute at work; though it is an appeal, not to another and perfect world, but to the natural harmony of man's activities before the event which distorted them to their present self-contradictoriness, the Fall. And the ground of the abjuration is just the pragmatical fact: repeated experience shows that sexual activity never actually yields the delight it promises, that it frustrates the mind and humiliates the body: indeed, it is possible that it irreparably harms life.

Donne's whole concern is the disparity between the necessary inadequacies of the act, as the distortion of man's nature at the Fall has left it, and the conditions necessary for the continuance of life; or to put it another way, the self-regulatory equipoise between men's appetites, and the anticipated mutilations which attend their indulgence. Men's desire to repeat the act, which is at bottom a haunting consciousness of brevity and a desire to prolong their own lives vicariously in their offspring, is always poised against the harm consequent upon its performance— the mental torpor, the humiliating loss of capacity, the physiological damage. To move from the *Vita Nuova* or the *Canzoniere* or *Astrophel and Stella* to this is to move to a different world; not a new or necessarily a more enlightened world, but emphatically one in which nature itself provides the norm, experience is the touchstone, and causal explanations precede final truths.

3. One world

A claim frequently repeated in the *Songs and Sonets*, with varying degrees of seriousness or extravagance, is crystallised in the conceit that lovers are a whole world to each other. It seems insufficient to treat as a bravura flourish or even a casual insight what does appear to be all of a piece with attitudes Donne quite consistently takes. Here too one sees a sharp if usually implicit rejection of courtly postures. For the idea that the mistress is the lover's world, in his eyes comprehending and far surpassing in herself all its wealth and dignities, was an old and important one; as was its complementary position, which Donne also takes, that all the lover's previous experience was an immature preparation for this, every previous attachment a partial anticipation of this. The difference is slight but decisive; it is that Donne supposes a shared experience. The use has turned from a device of idealised praise, a means of displaying devotion or suggesting beatification, to the delineation of a mutual relationship, an affirmation of the way things are between people in the world. A one-sided love is not truly love at all; the man's passion is mere adoration or admiration if it isn't given active point—'spheare'—by her love, and her love remains dormant until he activates it.

> Just such disparitie
> As is twixt Aire and Angells puritie.
> 'Twixt womens love, and mens will ever bee.
>
> (*Aire and Angels*)

Even at its most outrageous there seems more in this, as Donne uses it, than frivolous conceit; for what it conveys is not only an affirmation, but a judgment. Lovers who truly possess each other possess the world and are the world; indeed they are more than the world; and the world outside their love means nothing to them. And if the mistress and the lover between them comprehend in themselves all the world's riches, beauties, honours, then the traffic of the world, which turns on such things, is a deceit. Statecraft, commerce, nobility, are a mere play and mimicry, and the world's activity is nothing to their activity in bed, which is alone the truly serious business of human kind. At one level this is certainly standing things on their head, a way of quietly mocking the moral wiseacres who talk of love as a toy, to be put aside with youth for the serious business of life. But it is a judgment on that view, also, which some of Donne's finest poems defiantly or triumphantly proclaim. It isn't a mere tactical advantage which *The Anniversarie* works out but a personal affirmation with a claim to truth. Their love is alone exempt from time, and makes them unique, superior to all the world's honours and riches, and even to the sun; and their state here on earth now is superior to what it will be in the life of thorough but undiscriminated blessedness to come. The colossal hyperbole doesn't seem extravagant; its triumphant rhetoric pledges its fidelity to the lovers' feelings, and claims a more general validity too.

That this is a considered evaluation of experience *The Canonization* forcefully shows. If that splendid poem conveys anything beyond its lamenting outcry it is that love is a kind of religion, but a religion which ruins its devotees in terms of worldly success to *make* them in another and better sense. Such lovers must and do renounce the world and their own lives, for each other; love denies them the prizes of the world, but it gives them another superior world, with its own conditions and laws:

> Wee dye and rise the same, and prove
> Mysterious by this love.
>
> (*The Canonization*)

And again the 'mystery' is a human truth won through experience, the postcoital firmness which distinguishes this state from every other sexual relationship.

The proclamation of the last stanza specifically takes care of the possibility that all this is so merely in the sense that it has truth to these people's feelings in this situation. At one level, there is a consummation of the play of *religio amoris* on which the poem is built: these are love's martyrs, and saints, who can therefore intercede with the god himself on behalf of lovers still struggling for the heroic resolution to perfect their love. But the specific claim is that this love, already existing and just described, is the pattern or model of love itself. And if this is put forward as the necessary type or archetypal model of love, then the assertion seems to be that the truly perfected love is that which is prepared and firm enough to carry right through to the necessary extreme the conviction of its absolute paramountcy. Its special gift is the clearsightedness and resolution to put considerations of expediency and worldly career, not to say one's own life, after the simple human relationship, and accept the consequences.

Expediency was a necessary article of the courtly statute, of which this could be taken as a casual denial for the sake of paradox. It is certainly a denial, but not in fact casual here. The code Donne more specifically and pointedly puts against it emerges even in a genre piece like *The Dreame*, the rich history of whose central motif makes the tiny divergence all the more striking:

> Comming and staying show'd thee, thee,
> But rising makes me doubt, that now,
>   Thou art not thou.
> That love is weake, where feare's as strong as hee;
> 'Tis not all spirit, pure, and brave,
> If mixture it of *Feare*, *Shame*, *Honor*, have.

Her giving herself to him clandestinely is implicitly accepted as in no way inconsistent with the truth and sincerity he so warmly imputes to her. But love isn't consistent with her wish to conceal it. Real love, as we learn from *The Sunne Rising*, pays no more regard to fear, shame, honour, than to the traffic of the world of which these values are the preservatives, or to the seasons and climates which regulate that traffic. The appraisal is confirmed in *Breake of day*. There is a higher honour than Honour (reputation—the world's opinion), which consists in keeping faith with one's own truth, in standing by it and acting it out come what may. The secondary lesson of the emblematic shadows in *A Lecture upon the Shadow* is that it is an immature and still incompletely developed love that seeks to conceal itself. A mature love bravely eschews disguise, and makes all clear as it sees all clear; and that is its maturity. Pretence, deceit, disguise, concealment are finally incommensurate with an evaluation of human affairs which puts total dedication to a single human relationship before all considerations of expediency or prosperity, in this world or the next for that matter.

But *A Lecture upon the Shadow* carries a further lesson in its analysis of the condition of love's maturity. Love at the highest state of maturity— that in which it seeks no concealment, and everything is clear—can only be maintained so by continued absolute mutualness. The slightest disparity, an inappreciable diminution on either side, and deceit and falsehood swallow up all altogether. What one seems to be offered here is a harder lesson than the other, a stand against a different and subtler expediency. The terms express it modestly enough, but the demand implicit in them is uncompromising. It is not only 'fear' of others that is to be abjured, but 'fear' of each other. Mistrust, or uncertainty, or reservations, or incomplete confidence, no more go with love than does concealment; and so strictly is this the case that even the pretence of mistrust, for whatever reason, is to be avoided:

> True and false feares let us refraine,
> *(The Anniversarie)*

And the dramatic—almost melodramatic—enforcement of the point in the last line of *A Lecture upon the Shadow* is still harsher:

> And his first minute, after noone, is night.

The beginning of singleness is the instant end of love. With the starkness of that, as the lesson of experience, there is no temporising.

Conversely of course the condition for the perpetuation of a love which 'no season knowes, nor clyme,/Nor houres dayes, moneths', is an exactly and entirely reciprocal affection:

> If our two loves be one, or, thou and I
> Love so alike, that none doe slacken, none can die.
> *(The Good-morrow)*

While this mutualness persists, they have no need to fear or mistrust each other. And not only is the exemption of their love from the world's vicissitudes guaranteed, but they correct and stabilise each other; as in

E

the other condition they undo each other, mistrust and concealment breed mistrust and concealment. The best love is a love of souls so complete as to make one new and superior soul, which is then better than either was singly, and exempt from change; and this is a reciprocity which in fact guarantees mutual truth and stability even in physical separation:

> Thy firmness makes my circle just,
> And makes me end, where I begunne.
> (*A Valediction: forbidding mourning*)

From the natural morality and the psychology of love we are carried to the metaphysic of love, for which Donne is better known. Here again he takes over old fancies to make something at least very different, and possibly new. The figure of the stolen or strayed heart, and its refinements of exchanged, fused, and unified hearts all appear in the *Songs and Sonets*, often with very much the petrarchan force. But there appears to lie behind even these uses an appraisal of love which makes the figurative device less an extravagant fancy than the externalisation of a truth, and is always likely to dispel altogether the sense of a mere figurative play. What is at issue here finally, in the adjustments of the resolved figure, is the interinvolvement of mutual lovers, a notion often worked out in literal detail and with metaphysical consistency, but in a way that at times affords a genuine analysis of the condition it conveys. The lovers are so completely one that they are inter-affected and interdependent—they sigh each other's breath and the like. They have been fused by love into a new and superior soul, which is their whole being, so that separately they have no existence; from which it follows at one time that they have being only when they are together, as one entity, and at another time that their oneness is essentially undisturbed by mere physical separation. The sense spills over to the more directly petrarchan uses, to give them a substance which the sheer force of a poem often authenticates. The lover is so involved with his mistress that he is dependent upon her for existence, understanding, growth; he dies in absence from her; and his being is violently dissolved, annihilated, made nothing and the quintessence of nothing, by her death.

A distinction of Donne's use of these figures is that he tends to work out his materialisations in consistent metaphysical schemes, rather than in sequential anecdotes. This does afford a firmer appearance of intellectual authority than a mere anecdotal action could; but at best it has a more positive advantage in that the process itself is analytic and the feat of working it through offers him the possibility of an analysis of the condition his figure carries, a virtuoso opportunity which he splendidly uses. One recurrent preoccupation in these poems is the need to define love—a teleological exercise which at once provides a sharp insight and a clarification. The singularity of Donne's attitude here, which perhaps disingenuously suggests the ingenuous honesty of an inquisition absolutely rooted in his own experience, is his pragmatical refusal to commit himself to any positive assertion of motive and end. As with most of these professions, this can be handled more lightly or less. In *The Paradox* it is the basis of a paradoxical play: love cannot be defined, for either that is attempted without experience (and therefore vainly), or with experience, when by definition the attempted definer is already beyond speech, 'dead'. But there is more involved than a casual paradox. Even the lovers themselves, *A Valediction: forbidding mourning* tells us, don't know and can't define the essence of a love which has reached the highest degree; and as *The Extasie* implies, it is a mark of the highest love that it cannot be defined in terms of ends and motives.

The discrimination is precise, as one sees if one looks on the one hand at the attitude *Loves Alchymie* makes explicit, that it is a pitiful fable that 'not the bodies marry, but the mindes', and on the other at a poem whose subject is avowedly a special kind or degree of love. In *The undertaking* it is the very mark of the specifically platonic relationship described that motive and end are known and consciously maintained—a love of inward virtue. Here in fact one is shown the metaphysical basis of this attempt, the account of the character of things in scholastic terms of end and motive. Failing location of these, then an object can have no existence; or if it is known to exist, it must be beyond definition, as God is.

But this is meaningful for love too, as *Negative love* itself exactly demonstrates. In this poem, which calls on submissions Donne has made in a number of places through the canon, the inquiry after ends and motives is itself made overt, and the ground of the refusal to fix them clearly shown. Love is not fixed in sense, or in such faculties of the understanding as an admiration of virtue or the mind; for both sense and understanding know their proper end and the proper way to its attainment. Whereas the lover *does not know his own motives*, and so, repudiating all positive notions or assertions of specific end, can define love in no other way than by negatives. He knows what it is not, but he does not know what it is; and by implication, the inquiry itself is misconceived, for love is not an end-proposing activity, but a condition or state. Behind the bloodless movement of the academic processes, the sceptical mind pushes its rejections and negative gains through to a tested assurance, and repudiates alike the account of love as a motion of sense, and as a faculty of spirit in opposition to sensual lust. The assessment presents itself as an appeal from clear-cut logical categories, to the unresolved particularity of felt experience; and it recommends itself as a refusal to compromise one scruple of experience for a falsifying positiveness.

The careful negative discrimination of a 'refin'd' love is carried further in *The Relique*, where the situation seems generally akin to that represented in *The undertaking*; though the emphasis here falls on neither the heroic nor the self-denying aspects of the platonic relationship. In fact their condition is altogether nearer the regular one in that like the mature lovers elsewhere they were unaware of what they loved or why; and it is brought nearer still by the asseveration that this is good and faithful love. The difference lies precisely in the restraints this state distinctively professes: unconcern with difference of sex, no use of kisses save as salutation, and no availing themselves of the original natural freedom to enjoy physical love. But there is no condemnation here of sense, in fact quite the reverse. It is not for a moment claimed that this is the highest degree of love, and nothing in the poem suggests such a degree of mutualness; but only that there is a miracle of love at issue. And this appears to lie precisely in their abstinence from what is allowable, or at least ought to be allowed. The laws now governing physical relationships are not 'natural', since nature didn't impose them on the first men, but later arbitrary creations which injure nature; it is by the canons of this natural moralism, not by those of ascetic spirituality, that physical abstinence is a miracle of love. And strictly so; for a miracle is not a conformity with a denying ordinance, but an exception whose unique occurrence only confirms the law.

The 'law' for a mature love in fact, as Donne constantly reiterates it, is that this is a condition which makes no separation of the physical from the spiritual, bodies from minds. If a separation is made, it doesn't necessarily kill love altogether, but what ensues is so much less a complete love —as *The Blossome* lightheartedly implies:

As glad to have my body, as my minde.

This understanding of the relationship of body and mind in a good love has long been acknowledged as Donne's distinctive 'metaphysic', and it is very scrupulously defined in these poems. What his care was here one sees perhaps in a seemingly trivial adjustment of diction in *A Valediction: forbidding mourning*, a poem whose crux is the persuasion that physical separation is not separation at all, and whose overall sense would seem to be served by the unqualified urging of the pure union of minds. Donne does carefully plot for us the articles of his highest degree of love: this is the most refined love, of which there is an arcana, and a priesthood; it entails complete interassuredness of minds; and the one certainty the lovers have about its nature is the negative assurance that its essence is not sense. Physical contact thus is demonstrably not essential to it. But he will not say, as would precisely suit his overall argument, that sense has no place at all. It is 'Care *lesse*, eyes, lips, and hands to misse', where the 'lesse' marks at once scrupulous fidelity to the real sense of the situation, and a care not to concede lightly something of importance.

Loves growth, in its account of the augmentations of love, provides us with the morphology of the perfected state, as *The Extasie* gives us its economy. In *Loves growth* the sense is indirectly carried in the temporal metaphor, which depicts the passing of love from winter to spring, from one-sided adoration to the achievement of full reciprocity. Contemplation in winter; action—'Gentle love deeds', and heat—in spring. Love is deficient if it is only contemplative—if it concerns the mind or soul only; and by its nature requires a conjunction of contemplation and action, soul and sense. Love is not 'pure', but a mixture affecting or involving soul and sense together; and once sense, or mutual action, has been added to admiration to make up love, it will not be revoked again, but remains as a permanent gain, preserving the love thus consummated from any return of winter. Literally, this wholly mutual love is proof against diminution, withering, and death.

It is the office of *The Extasie* both to give metaphysical substance to the claim that love unifies and immortalises two souls, and to delineate precisely the relationship between soul and sense, mind and body in love; a continuous process which the dramatic setting, and the whole arrangement of the piece, seem to be cast to make as coolly direct and finely articulated as possible. In fact, even the minimal details of setting are made functional, emblematically; and the easy device of the bystander at once allows the conceit of love's arcana, and the more central suggestion that if 'good love' refines one to the point where one has grown all mind, there is a still further lesson to learn, through which the movement of the poem is to take us. The revelation vouchsafed the two lovers in the ecstatic departure from their bodies is the final knowledge 'Of what we are compos'd, and made'; and this is 'soules, whom no change can invade'. Essentially then the condition is a union of souls which has made them one new soul, exempt from the separate deficiencies of the single souls. None the less the matter can't be left there—'But O alas, so long, so farre/Our bodies why doe wee forbeare?' The union of souls is the essence; but it doesn't preclude the union of bodies as an accidental accompaniment, and for final fruition may require it. Physical union is not a necessary condition of the union of souls, nor is the union of souls itself incomplete without it. But without it, the new single soul suffers a mutilating deprivation. As the body is the active and operative agent of the soul, lacking which the soul would be bereft of all means of affecting the external world or communicating with it, so the joined bodies form the active and operative agent of the new single soul, without which the lovers could neither fructify their love, nor make it manifest:

> Else a great Prince in prison lies.

At one level the poem offers a considerable virtuoso play in Donne's manner of metaphysical conceit, very dexterously and consistently developed and clinched. At another, it can be seen as a kind of dramatised *cento* of attitudes and ideas about love developed in theoretical writings through the sixteenth century, notably in aristotelian Padua in opposition to the wholly transcendental tendency of Florentine neoplatonism. Undeniably it is a considerable intellectual performance; a virtuoso feat of wit, and a marvel of syncretic coherence. But as a poem, the record of a man's attempts to make sense of and be true to his own experience, it represents a significant event in the movement of European thought which is not likely to lose its force.

On the other hand, *The Extasie* need not at all represent John Donne's final utterance on the subject of love. That might equally well be *Loves Alchymie*, standing here as anti-type as *Farewell to love* stands against the ethic of the woman-hunt. It is another kind of dismissal of love. Love is a bubble, and the reputed pleasure of love is the shadow of a bubble. The conjunction of minds is a myth. Love has no essential end, and no central

happiness either; it is an imposture, promising much but yielding deri-
sorily little. Love is no refining experience but a squalid leveller, its
reward for initiate and clown alike no more than a humiliating coupling,
in which neither the act nor one's pleasure lasts more than a moment.
He is a fool who says that it is not bodies that marry but minds. Women
don't have minds. Even those who by some grace and life most suggest
mind are mere dead flesh when you have had them; and at the best time
in their lives, when they have at long last some sweetness and wit, they
are no more than dried-up flesh, activated demonically. Love, like the
alchemist, promises you the elixir and the philosopher's stone—eternal
life and the most precious of all things; and it gives you mummy, the
mere gummy scrapings of all that vast combustion, which at best
'Will cure the itch',[1] or have some momentary tang of sweetness about
it.[2] Against the presumption, the squalid and trivial reality; and the
truth is as you find it. Or more radically, human experience is equivocal,
there is no final certainty here.

5. *Wit*

Wit was not a revolutionary mode in lyric verse. It had been a feature
of Tuscan poetry from the thirteenth century, was prominent in
Petrarch's, and it dominated some later petrarchan schools. By the end of
the sixteenth century, indeed, there was a European literature of wit,
theoretically underwritten. For a poet, the decisive thing was what he
found in the store offered him, or could make of it. The drift of this
essay has been to suggest that Donne's wit is not arbitrary, or an enter-
taining embellishment; but that on the contrary, it is the mainspring of
his poetic method, and central to his poetic statement. One esteems him
as a poet, in the end, very much as one values his wit.

[1] Ben Jonson, *The Alchemist*, Act iv, Scene iii.
[2] See *O.E.D.* 'Mummy'. Senses of the word current in Donne's day
included 'dead flesh', and 'a medicinal preparation of the substance of
mummies, hence an unctuous liquid or gum used medicinally'. Donne's
poem is entitled 'Mummye' in almost all the early manuscripts.

Formally, the gain in the *Songs and Sonets* is at once a heightened mental exhilaration, and at least the appearance of an uncommon intellectual stringency. The dialectical arrangement of a poem, the habitual casting of an address in the form of reasoning processes, sets up an overall mental tension and gives strength and sinew to the intimate movement. A dramatic plot takes on a tighter-screwed cohesion in the pattern of premise and resolution; and the accompanying movement of 'If . . . then . . . except' also implies a keener discrimination—as it does in the technically comparable poetry of Michelangelo. With Donne even the lute-song pattern, vehicle of grace, is assimilated into the logical structure so that the refrain line is the announcement of the conclusion formally established, fixing the movement in tension with a decisive knot.

There is, moreover, the excitement as well as the satisfaction of things elaborately developed and exactly resolved. The purposeful evolution of a pattern, holding one through the slow unrolling of the figure, is answered by the conceited application; as in *A Lecture upon the Shadow* or *The Blossome*. Or the whole poem presents a developing argument which is clinched emblematically, or by chop-logic, in the very last line:

> Since thou and I sigh one anothers breath,
> Who e'r sighes most, is cruellest, and hasts the others death.
> > (*A Valediction: of weeping*)

Above all, and repeatedly, the ingenious elegance of fugue or an intricate deductive process is simultaneously a human insight.

Nor is this only a passive satisfaction. In *Loves Deitie* much quietly depends on the continual tension of positions announced, argued, and resolved, of expectation aroused and then satisfied. To observe one's response here is to find oneself engaged in a continuous dialogue, in which every statement sets up a fresh challenge or expectation, and the refrain-line comes as the key to a subtle process of keeping the reader guessing, offering now this way now that. Donne's figurative uses always invite the reading-in of correspondences, and the discovery of more. The initial analogy in *The Blossome* throws its properties forward very precisely. One is given an intricately exact analogue for a condition of love, which also exactly fixes an attitude, a distance; but it sets up its own tension, putting the onus on the reader to interpret and apply it, and positively spurring him on to the search for still more ingenious and recondite possibilities. This is a method which, beyond the poet's own coterie, is apt to leave a trail of cruces. In *Loves Alchymie* the central witty stroke is the submergence of the title-figure, after seemingly, incidental development, until the last line suggests in a single ambiguous appellation that it carries the whole point of the poem; and it takes on a sense that devastatingly clinches the play and the attack on women.

In the second stanza of *The Dreame* the poet at first takes the mistress's appearance to be an angelic visitation, though we know it is not. But her immediate behaviour demonstrates to us that she is truly angelic after all, in a precise and theologically accurate way; and then at once she shows herself still more than an angel in her specific capacity—a divine being. The conventional praise is twisted, twisted again, and then far exceeded; and each twist is really a richer life and meaning, a more human insight as well as a keener intelligence. Beyond adroitness, wit is here the nervous life of moving intelligence, and a sentience which is at once warm, and quick. There is the impression, too, in the packed subtleties which make up all these poems, of an alert and sensitively moving mind. Nothing is attitudinising or emoting, everything is nervously alive with various possibility; the issue seems the probing, testing, and extending of experience. And this is a live and flickering mental sensitivity that precludes set attitudes or predictable stances. Every piece seems a fresh response to immediate experience from the very midst of the experience itself.

It is the essential character of the *Songs and Sonets* to present not so much a single dominating feeling as a delicate complex of meanings, which, simulating a dramatic attitude, convey a mood or gesture more truly human in that it seems to seize on the kind of complexity life has, and that set stances often misrepresent. In place of a cry of passion one gets a reflection or inquiry whose processes seem to trace the movement of live human consciousness. This is a life which the most positive affirmation in no way stifles. The celebratory rhetoric of *The Anniversarie* comes as resolved assurance out of the witty to-and-fro of the whole movement; a confidence gained is at once seemingly betrayed, disturbing one's mind only to strengthen the final triumphant vindication. The impression of wary vigilance quite prevents the feeling that certainty has ever been too easily reached or an attitude allowed to harden; for the poet himself always seems to have taken more into account than the reader could have objected. A further effect of this much-qualified and life-packed movement is to suggest a more searching self-scrutiny. Nothing goes unsifted, everything is keenly and precisely discriminated; the mind is constantly at work, pondering, reconsidering, nagging it out. So that one distinction of the *Songs and Sonets* is the superior mental life they display.

The free-ranging life of *A Valediction: of the booke*, or *Song,* 'Goe, and catche', finds its expression not in the manipulation of neutral counters but in the pillorying of popular superstitions, learned chicanery, travellers' tales, and the crabbed disposition of the world in general. In place of a cold juggling with professional jargon or incompatible natural elements, such as petrarchan poets offer, we get a live bag of fools and rogues, whose recognisable aberrancies set us fairly and squarely in the common world of workaday instance and current report. The play presents itself less as the product of a desire to be witty, than as the reflex of an alert engrossment in daily affairs, and daily intellectual interests; the natural recourse of a mind to whom these things are alive, and matter, and whom presumably they may affect.

At the same time, there is a calculated irreverence that goes beyond a customary degree of satiric detachment. *The Apparition* is not only a piece of superbly blown-up viciousness but an exposé of conduct which implicitly debunks all the customary protestations and claims of lovers: hers, the new lover's, the poet's too. Witty extravagance here seems to turn back on itself—the comic extremes of the advances to love in *Loves exchange*, the grotesque disparity between the solemn urgency of the expostulations and the trivial object in *The Flea*, the absurd length to which the device is so gravely pressed in *The Computation*. In this highly conscious exaggeratedness there is an overtone of the ridiculous that derides the whole situation of attempts and resistance, and more directly exposes the typical attitudes struck. Beyond satire, it is the habitual self-mockery of the man who doesn't take himself or his subject over-seriously; and perhaps is to be taken the more seriously for that. So, frequently, with the exaggeratedly sceptical asides—'And my friends *curiositie*/Will have me cut up . . . .'.

The mocking womaniser's prayer to be preserved from loving, coolly inverting the usual order of values in love, makes *Loves Usury* a very different matter from the customary petition of the petrarchan abject. The effect is of a bargain lightly struck with an inferior, and carried through with cavalier offhandedness in the settlement of terms. In

Loves diet the ingenious subtlety of the stratagems described belies the overt humility of the address, or at least affirms a quite undaunted spirit in the face of power. This attitude to the tyrannous passion amounts to a refusal to take solemnly what becomes in this light humiliating and rather absurd. It is an affirmation of cool detachment and self-possession in the face of something that threatens independence, a stand against a commitment to one's own woes which disturbs normal poise and variety of response and congeals at worst into cold selfrighteousness. In one sense even the jaunty indifference of these dismissals could be accounted a more essentially serious attitude than the petrarchan; not more serious than, say, Dante's in his love-sonnets, but Dante has a moral substance that petrarchans rarely suggest. Hence the impression court-poets frequently give of preciosity, effeteness. Donne's stance may sometimes be flippant, even irresponsible by accepted standards, but it is masculine and it does take account of the real world.

It is an unsentimental acceptance of the way of the world that informs the cool temper and gentle reasonableness of a complaint like *Loves Deitie*, where the poet always seems detached or finally uncommitted behind it all, undeceived by his own rhetoric. This is the effect of the pattern of formal balance in *Womans constancy* also: the ironic import of 'one *whole* day' is mock astonishment, mock admiration, which the answering 'To morrow when thou leav'st' caps at once with a negligently sophisticated acceptance, indeed expectation of this ephemeralness. There is no more indignation or expostulation than there is pretence of smoothing things over, or of keeping up the fiction on which such affairs are usually founded—the vow his madly extravagant legal sophistries proceed to tear to shreds. That is the way things go, they both know it even when they don't admit it to themselves; so why make a fuss, or go through the motions of deceit! This is a realism constantly conveyed in mocking innuendo—'I *scarce* believe my love to be so pure . . .'.

The outright mockery of people and sects, and the impugning of motives in general, certainly isn't cynical. It expresses a perspective which takes the world's activities as ludicrous feverishness in respect of bedrock human certainties; not however occasion for despair, but diverting by their own zestful life. The overturning of accepted evaluations seems the more convincing because it is the reverse of solemn; and because it emphatically doesn't imply any rejection of experience, but rather a delight in it. This unawed assurance is the realignment itself, affirming a gay acceptance of the way things are, as well as a gay scepticism about what they claim to be.

Donne's wit exhibits a cool sanity and a wary openness which goes much beyond the refusal of facile commitments, or sardonic amusement at the way the world goes. It is the outward projection of a sense of the manysidedness of things, of manifold possibility; and ultimately a recognition of the multiplicity of experience. This comes through continually in the quizzing and weighing of everything, built into the poems in the characteristic formal movement—'For', 'So', 'Except', 'Thus'. Above all, it is a self-sifting. The internal dialectic of *The Blossome* enacts the continual suggestion of the relativity of its own affirmations, hinting even at a final questioning of the poet's positive stand. Awareness of his own pretensions and self-deceits motivates *Loves diet*, where the account of a self-imposed regimen, arising from a disinterested appraisal of his own condition, leaves one almost as conscious of the relativity of the position he finally reaches. And *The broken heart* does in fact make the opposite election, in a sifting movement which translates the poet's sense of his ambiguous predicament into dialectical complexity, a process at once keenly self-aware and aware of how things really are.

The assay is radical. The riddling movement of *The Message*, if it is anything more than frivolous, carries a dramatic searching of the ambivalence of motives, in which thwarted independence and an angry desire for revenge seem the necessary complement of love, and hopeless despair. But it also exhibits the ambiguity of the attachment itself. His eyes and heart, remaining voluntarily with her, presumably acquiesce in their own corruption and indeed attach themselves to her partly for that reason, whether the fascination lies in the conduct the poet complains of or in the personal character that manifests itself so. So that the contrary possibilities coexist in the same impulsion—love with bitterness, regard with disgust, and also the wish for independence with complete enthralment. One need not assume an immediate situation, or for that matter any direct expression of an actuality. It is just that the play isn't possible without a more than usually acute awareness of the ambiguity of motives and feelings; and the delineation of this is the movement of the poem.

The entire disposition of the *Songs and Sonets*, with its contradictions and distinctions and oppositions and utter disparities, testifies to the keenest sense of the manifoldness of experience. What one sees all the time are established certainties being crumbled, positive pretensions denied or mocked, the very affirmations of the poem doubted or discredited before it ends; and a few certitudes won by hard proof in the face of contingent circumstance. Here is a thoroughgoing relativism, confirmed as it seems by an acute personal sense of the relativity of claims and alignments. And this doesn't send one to 'new Philosophy'; save in so far as that is another claim, to be considered relatively as the rest. It is the naturalistic temper of many of the shrewdest Renaissance minds, as true to the nerve of later Renaissance life as the scepticism of Machiavelli or Montaigne, Rabelais or Aretino.

The representative use of these poems is the movement of *Loves exchange*, where the effect is of things coming freshly to mind, of attitudes modulating as new reflections occur, and as the conflicting emotions take him. Here one seems to find the complexity of things, immediately as they strike the moving intelligence; and the dialectical movement of the poem is no more than the shifting response to diverse experience. It is a shift which in the whole body of poems takes Donne through a conspectus of experiences of love, and likely as not leaves him reversing his bravest affirmations.

A Short Bibliography

The standard edition of Donne's poems are those by H. J. C. Grierson, *The Poems of John Donne* (Oxford, 1912) and by Helen Gardiner, *The Elegies and the Songs and Sonnets of John Donne* (Oxford, 1965). Grierson's edition is in two volumes, one of which contains a commentary on the poems. *The Songs and Sonnets of John Donne*, edited T. Redpath (1956) has close explanatory comments, poem by poem. Other editions which have notes on poems in the *Songs and Sonnets* are: *Metaphysical Lyrics and Poems of the Seventeenth Century*, edited H. J. C. Grierson (Oxford, 1921); *John Donne: Complete Poetry and Selected Prose*, edited J. Hayward (1929); *John Donne: Poetry and Prose*, edited H. W. Garrod (Oxford, 1946).

There is a bibliography covering all Donne's writings, by G. Keynes (3rd edition 1958), and a *Concordance* by H. C. Combs and Z. R. Sullens (Chicago, 1940).

The earliest life of Donne is that by Izaac Walton, 1640-75. E. Gosse's *Life and Letters of John Donne* (1899), though inaccurate, remains the standard account. There are short lives in E. M. Simpson, *A Study of the Prose Works of John Donne* (2nd edition 1948), and in the studies by K. W. Gransden and F. Kermode listed below.

The following are some of the numerous writings bearing on the *Songs and Sonets*:

S. Johnson, 'The Life of Cowley', in *Lives of the English Poets*, edited G. B. Hill (Oxford, 1905)

M. Praz, *Secentismo e Marinismo in Inghilterra* (Firenze, 1925). The first part of this essay was republished as *John Donne* (Torino, 1958)

P. Legouis, *Donne the Craftsman* (Paris, 1928)

T. Spencer (editor), *A Garland for John Donne* (1931)

T. S. Eliot, 'The Metaphysical Poets', in *Selected Essays* (1932)

J. Bennett, *Four Metaphysical Poets* (1934. Revised edition as *Five Metaphysical poets*, 1963)

M. Y. Hughes, 'Kidnapping Donne', in *Essays in Criticism, Second Series* (California, 1934)

F. R. Leavis, 'The Line of Wit', in *Revaluation*, 1936

C. S. Lewis, 'Donne and Love Poetry in the Seventeenth Century', and
  J. Bennett, 'The Love Poetry of John Donne', in *Seventeenth Century
  Studies presented to Sir Herbert Grierson*, edited J. Dover Wilson
  (Oxford, 1938)

R. Tuve, *Elizabethan and Metaphysical Imagery* (Chicago, 1947)

L. Unger, *Donne's Poetry and Modern Criticism* (Chicago, 1950)

J. B. Leishman, *The Monarch of Wit* (revised edition 1955)

K. W. Gransden, *John Donne* (1954)

C. Hunt, *Donne's Poetry: Essays in Literary Analysis* (Yale, 1954)

F. Kermode, *John Donne* (1957)

M. Praz, 'Donne's Relation to the Poetry of His Time', in *The Flaming
  Heart* (New York, 1958)

H. Davis and H. Gardner (editors), *Elizabethan and Jacobean Studies
  Presented to F. P. Wilson* (Oxford, 1959)

R. Ellrodt, *Les Poètes Metaphysiques Anglais* (Paris, 1960)

A. Alvarez, *The School of Donne* (1961)

F. Kermode (editor), *Discussions of John Donne* (Boston, 1962)

H. Gardner (editor), *Twentieth Century Views: John Donne* (New Jersey,
  1962)

A. Stein, *John Donne Lyrics's* (1962)